NOTORIOUSLY DAPPER

How to be a Modern Gentleman with
Manners, Style, and Body Confidence.

by
KELVIN DAVIS

Cover Design: Roberto Núñez
Layout & Design: Roberto Núñez

For permission requests, please contact the publisher at:
Mango Publishing Group
2850 Douglas Road, 3rd Floor
Coral Gables, FL 33134 USA
info@mango.bz

For special orders, quantity sales, course adoptions and corporate sales, please email the publisher at sales@mango.bz. For trade and wholesale sales, please contact Ingram Publisher Services at customer.service@ ingramcontent.com or +1.800.509.4887.

Notoriously Dapper: How to be a Modern Gentleman with Manners, Style, and Body Confidence.

Library of Congress Cataloging-in-Publication number: 2017952274
ISBN: (paperback) 978-1-63353-621-0, (ebook) 978-1-63353-622-7
BISAC category code:
SEL023000 SELF-HELP / Personal Growth / Self-Esteem
REF011000 REFERENCE / Etiquette

Printed in the United States of America

Table of Contents

Introduction

"Every dream starts with a vision.
Every vision begins with a passion.
Every passion starts with love."

– Notoriously Dapper

On September 10, 1987, a boy was born in Columbia, South Carolina. Little did he know what life held for him, how blessed he would be, and how much love he would share with the world. That little boy grew up to be me. Hey, for those who don't know me, I'm Kelvin C. Davis II, the creator and founder of Notoriously Dapper, a body positive men's style blog. I have always been fascinated with art and fashion – seeing pictures of really well dressed people always intrigued me. I have always felt that pictures say so much more than words. Style can do the same. So naturally, when you add them both together, they evoke an array of feelings, thoughts, and words that come to mind. The story of my 30-year journey to becoming a body positive gentleman will hopefully help you embrace your own journey and find the beauty in the struggle. There have been plenty of books written about etiquette for men; you may ask, what makes mine different? That's a good question. My perspective is what makes this different. Let's face it; I'm a young, black, male millennial. Although I have been blessed with parents who are amazing, loving, and supportive, simply being who I am in society has been rough for me some days.

Growing up in the white suburbs of Irmo, South Carolina, caused some confusion for me. People would often tell me that I talked "white" and dressed "white." I didn't really understood what that meant until my middle school years, when I moved to Orangeburg for two years (7th and 8th grade). Being constantly told that I didn't act "black" was kind of confusing for me. I mean, I listened to rap music, I could dance, and I was clearly black. But for some, I guess I was never "black" enough. During this time, I was also shopping in the "husky" section. My mom would make it seem special, as if it was this exclusive shopping club for cool kids. She has a way of making me feel better about things. I remember in middle school, a girl told me she liked my jeans! I was excited because she was one of the "popular" girls and was super sexy. She asked where I got them from, and I told her with all the pride in my voice, "These are from the "husky" section." She laughed and said, "You mean the fat boy section?" I was like, "Nah, the husky section." She then notified me that "husky" was a nice way of saying "fat boy."That was my first time being called fat, and I have to admit it hurt me. I felt shamed and didn't want to shop in the husky section anymore. My love for clothes and fashion was still there, but it couldn't emerge in full force due to my size at the time.

By high school, I had grown some and was able to shop in "normal" stores. My mother went to Myrtle Beach one weekend for a work conference. While she was there, she bought me a pink polo shirt from the Ralph Lauren outlet store there. It was a bright fuchsia pink, and I LOVED IT. I had never seen any guy wear that style of shirt before, and I was super excited to be one of the first at my school to rock it. I ironed it, hung it up, and waited for Monday to come so I could straight UP stunt on these students. Monday came, I got dressed for school, and I was rocking the pink polo. I got onto my bus, and everyone was like, "DAMNNNNNNNN, that's dope. Where did you get that shirt?" I was feeling myself at that moment, and for the first time I felt CONFIDENT AF. Of course I had some haters that said stuff like, "That's a faggot color," or my personal favorite, "You know that's a girl shirt, right?" But the girls LOVED me for wearing it. I got all the attention that day, and it helped boost my self-confidence. I wore the collar popped up also; I was still kind of chunky and had some rolls in my neck. So I popped the collar to hide them a little bit. Unbeknownst to me, there was a musical artist who was on the come-up wearing the same type of clothing and colors that I was wearing: Kanye West. The more I wore these bright-colored polo shirts with the collar popped, the more I got noticed for my broad and fearless sense of style. I went from being a middle school "husky" kid to being a high school fashion trendsetter. People nicknamed me "Kanye East," 'cause we had the same swagger at the time. When I started following Kanye and what he was doing in hip-hop, it dawned on me that I was doing the same thing, but in high school on a smaller scale.

You see, before Kanye, a lot of rappers and hip-hop artists dressed in long white tees and oversized street wear. He came out of nowhere with this college prep type swag and turned the game upside down, the same way I did when I wore that fuchsia pink polo with the color popped. That day set the tone for how I dressed in life. I had always been afraid of wearing certain things in middle school because of my size. But when I got to high school, I wore what I wanted to wear, when I wanted to wear it. This helped me develop the fearless fashion sense I have today. I'm one of the biggest Kanye West fans because of this. I feel as of we have lived parallel lives for quite some time. There wasn't any role model for me growing up – I didn't have any body icons or fashion icons. The only black male model I remember as a kid was Tyson Beckford. Little did I know all of this would come full circle for me.

Now that we live in a digital age, it's a lot easier to put who you are, your journey, and your story out there. When I created Notoriously Dapper, I not only wanted to show off my style as a "bigger" guy, but also to create that role model that I didn't have growing up. Everywhere we look, it's about getting lighter, getting thinner, and meeting an unrealistic standard of beauty that doesn't exist in the real world. I recall being in that "husky" section and looking at the ads for the other departments, wondering, "Why can't I have abs?" "Why can't I have blonde hair?" or "Why can't I have blue eyes?" I remember not knowing that who I was and how I looked was good enough. Now, I know that. I have a responsibility to share my body struggles with you all, to share the need for more diversity in the media and fashion industry. We all need representation of some kind.

Representation is everything. We are slowly losing our young men and women to reality television and what they see on the internet. People have forgotten what it is to be nice, to be caring, to love uncondishy (you will learn what this means later), and to live their own life. In this book I will share my journey with you on how I became a modern gentleman with manners, style, and body confidence. Am I an expert? No, but these stories I share with you are 100% true, and it brings joy to my heart to share them. These past 30 years of my life have been quite the time. Time flies, but the good news is you're the pilot. So strap yourself in, grab a beer or wine, and enjoy.

By the way, before we get started, let me tell you this... you're beautiful. Don't let anyone tell you different. Your body isn't wrong, the media is. Now turn this page so we can get it started. Let's get it started in here...and the bass keeps runnin' runnin' runnin'. Okay, sorry, I couldn't resist singing those Black Eyed Peas lyrics. Now for real...let's get started.

Dedication:

This book is dedicated to my father, the man who raised me to be who I am today. You're the definition of manners, style, and body confidence. Thank you for being the best Dad a boy could ask for. This one is for you, I love you.

My Dad and I at my first birthday party! #TBT

Chapter 1

Gentleman, Redefined

"You can pay for school but you can't buy class."

- Jay-Z

Living in the modern world with new ways of communicating and interacting can be a bit stressful. Back in the 1950's, people didn't have to worry about cell phones, social media, and the heavy tension the media causes in our society. Men in that day behaved differently because of the time period, although I'm sure there were jerks then as there are now. What's the difference now? Well, the difference is that everything we say and do can be put on the internet for the whole world to see in just a matter of seconds. That's the downfall and beauty of living in a digital age. We all know that racism, sexism, and bigotry existed before the technological era, but it was easier to ignore, because we never experienced it the way we do now in this digital day and age. Everything from the way we communicate to the way we live has been redefined over time, so it's only natural that the term "Gentleman" has to be redefined as well.

What is a Gentleman? Do they exist? How do I spot one in this modern day? These are all questions people ask themselves and others daily. Acting in a gentlemanly way has become so rare that a lot people mistake it for flirting or being creepy. What's so creepy about buying someone's coffee with no intention of wanting anything in return? Nothing is creepy about it. What's creepy is that people have become so accustomed to others always having ulterior motives that they can't simply appreciate a gentleman's nice gesture. And don't get me wrong, you don't have to buy a stranger coffee to be a gentleman. What makes you a gentleman in the modern day is simply being thoughtful, aware, loving, understanding, tolerant, and KIND! It's hard to be considered a gentleman if you are lacking any of these qualities. So I'm going to break down each characteristic and give you some examples. Most of these examples are true situations from my life or that of someone I know. Brace yourself, 'cause it's about to get real for you ladies and fellas.

"Thoughtful" by definition means showing consideration for the needs of other people. The key word in there is OTHER people – which is someone other than your damn self. Don't be selfish and always think about what you want, need, and deserve. Believe it or not, others, especially your loved ones, have wants and needs and are deserving. We all have parents or guardians who looked after us when we were growing up and being foolish. It's not till we get older that we see the sacrifices, hard work, and thoughtfulness they always were demonstrating. All the days when bills were stacked up to their head, work was at an all-time high, and they were full of frustration, their only concern was making sure you were taken care of and happy. As a father, I now understand more of what it is to be thoughtful. It's not about me; it's about them (my daughters). It's about their smiles, their tears, their fears, and their needs – not mine. It's your job as a gentleman to showcase this type of thoughtfulness so we can build better communities for our children. Being thoughtful is more than just looking after people you know. Helping strangers can go a long way.

I was taking my family to go grab some dinner from Five Guys. While driving, I hit this major pothole – it flattened my front passenger tire and bent my back passenger rim up pretty bad. I pulled over to take a look at the damage, and then started getting the supplies out to change my tire. While I was changing my tire, a man who lives across the street came over and asked me if I needed help. I said, "Yeah, I do. My lug wrench is stripped and it won't latch on." He then not only stopped mowing his lawn to get me a lug wrench, but he brought out something to drink for me, and for my wife and girls, because it was clearly hot outside and I was sweating it up trying to change this tire. He was thoughtful. As he helped me take the lug nuts off and put the spare tire on, I began to realize how rare this moment was – a middle-aged white man helping a young black man change a tire. Not only did he help me, but we also had a great conversation about Gamecock football, boiled peanuts, and Five Guys. We introduced our families to one another, gave thanks, and hugged goodbye. It was a great moment for my daughters and his son to see that helping people is okay and that it's encouraged. He could have easily turned the other cheek, gone into his house, and not offered me a single helping hand, but he did the opposite. He was being a gentleman by offering a helping hand; regardless of whether I accepted it or not, he did his part by being thoughtful.

Having knowledge or perception of a situation or fact can save you from getting into trouble and help you stay afloat in your day-to-day life. When you are aware of things, you tend to make more reasonable decisions than those who are unaware. Being aware is a very useful character trait in becoming a gentleman. If you are aware that holding the door for someone who is directly behind you is gentlemanly, then chances are you will hold the door open for them. Building awareness takes time and consideration. It's not something that will happen overnight, and we all have different perceptions of situations. But your awareness must be able to keep people safe while not harming others. When you have knowledge of something, it's always nice to share it as well. Sharing your awareness about topics will help give others insight and a different and new perspective.

Love is what makes the world go around. Loving someone can change his or her life and yours. Often when people speak of love, they assume "romance," but there are more types of love than just romantic love. Loving someone is simply showing that you care about them. We are taught at a young age to love our family, friends, and mankind. It is okay for anyone to love, whether it's romantic or not. Love is universal, it has no color, sex, or boundaries. It is one of the purest emotions we have as humans. Why is love an important characteristic for being a gentleman, though? It's simple: because without it, you're an asshole. Yeah, that's right. If you can't love, then chances are you are a mean individual, which automatically takes you out of this gentleman's game...so good-bye and have a nice life, sir. Wait, you still want to play? You want to learn how to love? Oh, well okay. First start by loving yourself – if you can do that, then you can love anybody. Find the good in people and embrace it. We all love for different reasons, but no one should love someone with an intention of gaining by it. Your love should be unconditional at all times.

I learned about unconditional love through my aunt (my mom's sister); when I was a kid, she would always say to us, "I love you", and we would of course reply, "I love you too." But the best part was when she would get close to you and say, "How much you love me?" and we always said, "Uncondishy." We (my sister, my cousins and I) were very young and clearly couldn't pronounce unconditional correctly yet. I knew what it meant even at that age, it meant that I loved her no matter what she did or happened. If our love has conditions, then we can't grow and accept other humans for what we are, which is imperfect beings. We are perfectly imperfect. When we choose to love a friend, colleague, family member, or partner we have to be prepared to love them "Uncondishy" – yeah, that's right, I'm starting a new word trend. When I say "Un" you say "Condishy" – UN-CONDISHY, UN-CONDISHY. Loving someone that way allows you to embrace their flaws just as much as their positive attributes. Don't worry, you've got a lot more coming about love, so let's leave it here for now, shall we.

Be understanding of the fact that people have differences. Be tolerant of those differences, and be kind to everyone. Listen, look here...I said look. We all have differences; we come from different backgrounds, cultures, and societies. So chances are someone you meet isn't probably going to agree with you on everything, and that's okay. When I transferred to the University of South Carolina in the spring of 2007, I got put in a dorm room with a roommate I didn't know. I wasn't worried about it at all; I can get along with just about anyone. I showed up on move-in day and there he was, a straight-up country boy from Tennessee. I walked in and saw a huge confederate flag, Navy SEAL decals, and Jack Daniels bottles everywhere. He was sitting shirtless with a cowboy hat on, playing on his laptop. He got up with a huge smile on his face and reached out and shook my hand. He said, "You must be my new roommate!" Yes, I was his new roommate. I'm not even going to lie, I came up with all sorts of assumptions about him, including that he was probably racist and didn't like black people at all. My mom, being from the country herself, said, "He just likes to drink and have fun. He doesn't care what race you are." That clearly didn't change my skepticism about him at all. As Taylor and I began living the college life together, we bonded and became friends. He got me drunk for the first time off his favorite drink, which was whiskey sours, and also took care of me when I was hung over the following day. We never talked about race issues or his confederate flag. It didn't bother me because I knew his heart as a person.

As time went on, we became a lot closer. So close in fact that when I came back one day from class, his confederate flag had been taken down and replaced with an American flag. Mind you, I never once mentioned the fact that it bothered me ever. I was curious after I initially saw it, and asked him why he took it down. He said to me, "Because I saw your face when you first came here, and I wanted you to feel comfortable living with me." He didn't have to do that, but he chose to because it was thoughtful. In my heart, I was comfortable living with him; all my assumptions had already been dismissed because of the way he treated me. When the school year was about to come to a close and final exams were upon us, we didn't see each other for a few days; pulling those all-nighters was a struggle. One night he texted me and said, "I've got to tell you something when you get back to the dorm." I was studying in the bottom floor of the Thomas Cooper library, which meant no cell phone signal. So when I resurfaced above ground from the library to head back, I checked my phone and saw that text. I was thinking 'Damn, he's not coming back next year." I walked in. and he said, "Man, listen – your girlfriend is cheating on you." I was like "WHAT?! How do you know?" He said, "She's sleeping with one of my navy friends' roommates."

Long story short, I broke out in an instant rage. I started calling her, while panicking and pacing. It turned out to be true. I broke down; he calmed me down, offered me a drink, and we talked. The next day, I broke off contact with her after two years of dating. But it was okay, I may have lost a girlfriend, but I had gained an amazing friend. We kept in contact throughout college, and I ended up being one of his groomsmen in his wedding. He is happily married with a beautiful baby boy, and although we don't talk a lot at all, I wish him nothing but the best in life. He's an amazing human being. Despite our differences he treated me like a brother. He was thoughtful, aware, loving, understanding, tolerant, and kind, a true gentleman...a southern gentlemen.

The 6 Essential Assets of a Redefined Gentleman

1. Being thoughtful requires you to actually think. Think about others and yourself. It's okay if you do things to look out for your own best interest, but always remember that thinking of others goes a long way as well. We often hear, "It's the thought that matters most." Well, it's true; people genuinely recognize when someone is being thoughtful, when you go out of your way to do something for someone. When you buy a stranger coffee with the intention of wanting nothing in return, that's being thoughtful. Thoughtfulness comes in a variety of ways. Find what being thoughtful is for you and apply it to your daily interactions, relationships, friendships, and more. You will see the effect it has on yourself and others; the impact of being thoughtful is unforgettable.

2. Awareness is more than just noticing something; being aware has a sense of understanding. We are all aware of our feelings, surroundings, perceptions, and thoughts. Being aware in your daily life can help you and others live more freely. When you are aware you tend to be more "woke," which means you have a sense of what is going on in the world and in today's society. For me, being a black male, I'm aware I can't do half the things my white counterparts do. That's the reality we are living in. Taylor was aware that the confederate flag could offend me, although I never mentioned anything about it. He took it down; he

took it down because of his awareness of the harm it could bring to others. It takes a true gentleman to take such an action. Awareness is one thing, but acting on it is another. Act on your awareness, be proactive, and keep making this world a better place.

3. The act of showing love is being loving. People always think that you can only show love in a romantic way. Cancel that noise right now! You can show love to anyone, strangers, family, wife, and so forth. Yes, there are different forms, types, and intensities of love, but nonetheless you can show love to anyone. Bosses show love by giving raises, awards, or recognition. Simply being kind shows love to everyone, I mean, you can't say being kind is a form of hate, right? We all are born with love in our hearts, then as we get older life experiences increase or decrease our love. It's unfortunate, but there are people in this world who don't have human compassion and love for all. That's why as a redefined gentleman you need to keep that in mind and always be kind to others. You never know what a kind loving gesture may do for someone, it could give someone hope that there are good people out there in this world. Show love daily to yourself and others.

4. Understanding is deeper than just listening or paying attention. Putting yourself in someone else's place or circumstance helps you understand. Acting on that understanding elevates who you are as a person. Some naturally understand from their own life's experiences and others have to become understanding. If you are

driving to work and you get a flat tire, you would hope that your boss or supervisor would understand your dilemma. Believe it or not, there are plenty of people who are not understanding until they need someone to be understanding of them. Our boss or supervisor isn't immune to flat tires, getting sick, etc. That's why it's so important to always be understanding of every circumstance, because it could happen to you. As a husband and father you get a whole new sense of understanding. When you become a husband, you have to understand that it's not just about you anymore; you have another person who is a part of your life. The decisions you make can not only affect you but affect them as well. Being a dad requires the strongest amount of understanding ever – you have got to be able to understand why it's important for you to be around, how to make them smile, and correct them when they are in the wrong, but most importantly, show them how to love others. It's a big responsibility and it's not for everyone, but if you can do it while understanding the importance of being a good person, then you, my friend, have got this on lock.

5. Tolerance is a virtue; when one is tolerant of others then they can live freely. We live in a world where millions of people have different religious views, sexual orientations, and ways of living their own life. We cannot be distracted by all the bullshit and forget to be tolerant of one another. Just because someone loves differently than you, does not mean

you should judge them, shame them, or attack them. We have seen what intolerance can do to a country. It can hurt or kill, and it can damage an entire society. We have to rise above and promote the tolerance of our differences. It's the only way we can function as a world, we are not always going to see eye to eye or listen ear to ear. But we can agree to live our lives the way we want to without anyone telling us the opposite. Let other people do them, you do you. It's that simple; keep it one hundred percent all day long. Tolerance can set us free, when we learn to be tolerant of others then we can truly live as one.

6. Last but surely not least is kindness. Kindness is always the answer, *always*. If you can't be kind, then the first five essentials are going to be difficult for you. Kindness is the foundation for all of this. I mean what are thoughtfulness, awareness, love, understanding, and tolerance without kindness? Nothing, it is simply nothing but a bunch of empty false actions that mean shit. That's the honest truth; you can say what you want. Without kindness all of this means nothing. Anything you do needs to involve kindness. When you're being thoughtful, be thoughtful with kindness. When being tolerant, be tolerant with kindness. Be loving, understanding, and aware with kindness. Kindness is the foundation of all improvement in our character.

Dress well. Be nice. Smile. Repeat.

We ain't picture perfect but we're worth the picture still. #JCole

The clothes don't make the man. They just help him look better. #Facts

Chapter 2

Gentleman Gestures

"More poise, less noise."

- Dwayne "The Rock" Johnson

There are 7.4 billion people who live in this world, and chances are we all have encountered some type of good deed from someone. It's safe to say that if all 7 billion people were selfish and only thought about themselves, we would live in a pretty screwed-up world – a world where leaders never did anything to benefit their citizens, teachers never taught students, and so forth. We need people who have a kind spirit and want to help others. Help is what makes this world go around. As a man, asking for help or accepting help doesn't make you weak in any way, shape, or form. If anything, it shows that you're open-minded to the fact that someone could help you accomplish something you had trouble with. Little things like holding the door open for someone, giving up your seat on the subway, or even providing a listening ear to someone in distress can go a long way to help.

I touched on the characteristic of being aware in the first chapter. Being aware is going to help you become more selfless and kind. I was grocery shopping one day (which I rarely do) and couldn't help but realize how many assholes there are in this world. It quickly reminded me why I don't go grocery shopping often. People had their carts in other people's way, no one would say excuse me, and worst of all, some entitled folks were cutting the deli line. Look, it doesn't take much to say excuse me, please, and thank you....a damn THANK YOU! People work very hard at their jobs and deserve a "thank you" for serving you.

The most pleasant part about my grocery fiasco was checking out. This was not because I was leaving that hellhole, but because the cashier and the bagger were simply amazing. The cashier asked me how my day was going, and I said great. We had a brief conversation about the erratic behavior of the customers. He laughed during our talk and said, "We call it power hour, because for some reason, around this hour people are just powering their way through here with a purpose." He was right. They were all in a rush and just simply forgot to be nice, I assume. As he was scanning my items, a male bagger came up and started bagging my groceries with a smile that could brighten up the darkest place in the world. His name was Cole (according to his badge), and he was full of life. He talked to me about football and what he planned on doing after he got off work. After bagging all my groceries, he offered to help load them up in my car. Although I declined, it was the thought that mattered to me. The simple act of kindness and thoughtfulness of offering a helping hand was enough.

As I was walking to my car, I saw a pregnant lady with her two toddlers who was clearly struggling to load her groceries into her car drop her keys on the ground. I was on the other side, so I figured someone closer would surely be kind enough to pick her keys up for her. I saw a guy walk by and say to her, "Ma'am – you dropped your keys there!" and then keep walking. I was thinking, "What the hell just happened?" He had just told a pregnant woman with two kids that her keys had fallen and then didn't even think to help her pick them up. Thankfully, the (female) person right behind him picked them up for her. But I began to wonder why someone would do that. I mean, it's a simple gesture that could have helped her a lot. Maybe no one had ever taught him to do such a thing, maybe he'd had bad experiences with helping others, especially women, or maybe he was just being an asshole. I don't know what his reasoning was, but I do know if he had just picked up the keys for her, it would have helped her a great deal.

It got me thinking back to when I would make such gestures and people thought I was flirting with them. Yes, being nice has become so uncommon that some people mistake it for flirtation. I can name countless times that I have complimented someone and they replied, "I have a boyfriend". Huh....okay, thanks for the memo, I have no interest in you whatsoever and I apologize for liking your floral dress. Believe it or not, ladies, a man can admire something about you without wanting to have sex with you, be with you, or even have ill intentions. When someone compliments the aesthetics of a building, no one says, "Well, the building isn't interested in you;" it's an irrelevant remark to something innocent and genuine. I'm simply saying, don't take a compliment solely as someone's way of being attracted to you. A lot of guys like myself who like art and fashion and have a creative mind don't compliment you to hit on you. Take it as a nice thoughtful comment, say thank you, and keep it moving.

I believe that many men lack gentlemanly gestures for two reasons; one, people take it the wrong way, which causes some men to stop wanting to be a gentleman because they see no reward in being one, and two, that they were never taught how to make such gestures. Either way it goes, we need more gentlemanly gestures in this world. All in favor, say "Aye"...I can't hear youuuuu, I SAID all in favor say "AYE!" I know we have all heard the term "pay it forward", meaning do something nice for a random stranger and they will then hopefully feel the kindness of it and do the same for someone else. It's a pattern that helps the world work a bit better in these rough days.

I personally grew up watching this take place in my household. I remember as a kid seeing my dad buy other people coffee, adopting families during Christmas, and always encouraging my sister and me to do likewise if we could. When I was a sophomore in high school, I remember riding with my dad to the gas station one day to get a soda and fill his tank up. There was a man there who had run out of gas and unfortunately didn't have any money on him to get more gas. It seemed like he had been out there for a while, from the look of frustration and desperation on his face. He walked up to my dad and explained to him what had happened to his wallet; my dad replied, "Say no more, I will put ten dollars' worth in for you." This man's face lit up with relief and hope. He expressed how thankful he was and how he had been dying to get home. That moment stuck with me even till this day.

Fast forward to nine years later when my wife and I had just bought our first house. We were new to the neighborhood and really didn't know anybody. My daughter was playing out in the front yard while my wife was doing some gardening when a man with a wet shirt asked her if we had a gas canister. My wife came in and asked me if we had one. I told her no, and she asked me to go outside to talk to this gentleman. I could see why my wife would be alarmed, he looked unkempt, sloppy, and a bit unusual to say the least. He began telling me that he had lost his wallet and had run out of gas, et cetera et cetera et cetera. I didn't believe his story enough to help him. He said thank you and continued walking to find help. As I began walking back into my house, my gut intuition started to speak to me, and reminded me of when my dad had helped out that guy at the gas station.

I went inside, grabbed my keys, got in my car, drove around the block, and told him to hop in. A part of me was thinking, "Kelvin, what in the hell are you doing? This man could be a serial killer." But I had a good feeling about him after my intuition kicked in. I took him to the gas station, which was right around the corner; I went in and bought a gas canister to fill up with gas for him. As I was filling up the gas can, he began telling me how much he appreciated me having a change of heart. I said it was no problem and told him the story about my father. He said to me, "You learned by example to help others, that's all right," and he was right – I did learn from that example.

I gave him the canister and asked if he needed a ride to his car, he told me no, that it was right across the street. He gave me a side "man hug" and said thank you again. It was no problem for me to help him out. I had peace of mind knowing he was able to get where he needed to go. If he is ever confronted with the same dilemma one day, I'm sure he will help someone in need as well. That's what paying it forward is all about; my dad did it, so I did it as well. It's a chain reaction of positive energy that makes the world a much more loving place.

We all appreciate positive vibes, and doing nice things creates those vibes. Despite how people may react to you being nice, continue to have faith in humanity. You can't worry about how someone will react when you're being nice. That's out of your control. I remember when I first visited New York City and I held the door open for someone, they said to me, "You think I can't open the door for myself?" Instead of getting upset, I just smiled at him. See, we never know what kind of day people are having. They could be having the worst week ever, though that still does not excuse their actions. It's never okay to be a jerk in any situation; always remain positive even when the other party isn't.

A huge part of becoming your own man, especially a gentleman, is learning how to deal with negativity. One of the downfalls of being well-known on social media is that you often deal with "internet trolls". Don't know what they are? Let me explain. An internet troll is someone who usually spends much of their time on the internet behind a username saying rude, absurd, disgusting, and hateful things to other internet users. How we respond to them shows what kind of people we really are. If we attack back with the same hate and vengeance, then that defeats the purpose of us being role models. It's when we either don't respond or respond with care that it throws them off. They want you to get mad and fight fire with fire. I want you to think of yourself as water when fighting with fire, use the water to dilute the fire. Don't let the negativity of others bring down your positivity, don't let another person break you out of your composure. It's important to remember this, because you could lose your reputation or respect from "blowing your top", and no one wants that to happen to them.

In a world full of fuck boys, be a gentleman. Hold that door for the person behind you, buy a stranger some coffee just because it's a beautiful day outside, pick up those keys someone dropped and hand them, and most importantly, forget those haters. You never know when you may need the favor returned – keep being positive, and when you least expect it, at the time when you're in need, you will get that help of positive energy. It will rain on you like a summer day in Seattle (I don't know if that's an actual saying or not, but it sounds hella fresh). Day by day, if we continue to build each other up with love and random acts of kindness, we will make this world a more amazing place. Trust your gut, use water to fight fire, and keep your composure. Everything else will fall into place...trust me, I'm a living example.

11 Traits Every Modern Gentleman Should Have

1. Have a good sense of humor, laugh at things every once in a while. As the saying goes, sometimes you have to laugh to keep from crying. People love a good sense of humor and someone who can make light of a situation to take pressure off others. Be that comic relief for someone, we all need that.

2. Be open-minded and a constant learner. Don't think you know everything, because chances are you will come across someone who knows more than you, and that's okay. Instead of being intimidated by someone's intelligence, just simply learn from them. Mental growth is all about having that continuous thirst for more knowledge; whether it be about women, art, science, or cars, we could all use a new lesson every now and then.

3. Punctuality and promptness are key when arriving somewhere important, like work, a date, or a dinner engagement. Always try and make time to be somewhere early, being early looks a lot better than being late. When you are prompt and on time, people see that as an indicator of caring and wanting to be there. And as the old saying goes, the early bird gets the worm!!

4. Do your part to maintain a healthy conversation when talking to others. More goes into holding a great

conversation than people think. Giving someone your undivided attention while conversing is one of the most respectful things you can do, and it doesn't involve much effort at all. Be a good listener and responder, make sure you are paying attention to what they are saying. In conversation, there is nothing worse than asking someone a question, then seconds later having to repeat it again. Being responsive to what someone says not only shows that you're listening but that you care about what they are saying. Always remember to make eye contact, listen, and respond – this will maintain great conversations for people to remember you by and build relationships.

5. Smile more, especially when out and about. Nothing is more heartwarming than seeing a genuine smile on someone's face. Also, try to make others smile by being nice and courteous. Positivity radiates through people and inspires us all to be better. Making someone smile can bring joy to your heart and make you smile as well. Many say I have a smile that could brighten up the darkest valleys, and a compliment like that makes me smile even more!

6. Being well-mannered is one of the most important traits of being a gentleman. Opening the door for someone, waiting to eat until your other guests have been served, walking to your date's door, and speaking politely are all different ways you can show your manners. Dressing well is also a form of good manners. When you dress well for something like a date or a work or family function, you are showing

those in attendance that you not only care about yourself, but that you have enough manners to dress for the occasion. Be the guy that everyone looks forward to seeing when you show up!

7. Be non-judgmental, non-racist, non-homophobic, and non-misogynistic. To me there is nothing worse than someone who views themselves as superior because of their financial status, race, religion, gender, or sexual orientation. This is unacceptable and inexcusable. This does not even need to be drawn out in detail for you. If you have a problem with people because of their race, financial status, religion, gender, or sexual orientation, then you are NOT a GENTLEMAN! In order to be a gentleman, you need to accept everyone. I didn't say AGREE with everyone, I said ACCEPT everyone. We are all different, but we are all human beings and should be treated as such. Having love for humanity is the most important trait to have as a gentleman.

8. Be confident but humble. Confidence is beautiful and always helps in conquering the obstacles in life, but cockiness will get you in a place where no one wants to be. It's okay to have confidence in your ability to do something, but always be humble enough to know that someone out there is always better. Be the best *you* can be and don't worry about others. My dad used to tell me, "Nothing is more humbling than life itself." It's true, we are never promised our health, life, or current situation, so always be thankful. Staying humble is a way of being thankful for what you have

accomplished in life. Continue to be confidently humble and the path to success will be yours, with some hard work along the way.

9. Decisiveness is a great trait to have as well. Take control of your life, body, and career! Think about it this way, it's either one day or day one. We all have those "one day" moments, like one day I'm going to open that coffee shop, one day I'm going to wear this outfit, one day I'm going to start a fashion blog, or one day I'm going to love myself. Instead of saying one day, say day one. Today is day one of loving myself, day one of my coffee shop opening, day one of my fashion blog, and this is day one of me wearing this outfit! Day one means you have made a decision to go ahead and follow that passion and take control. Be decisive and own who you are.

10. Practice good grooming habits. Some men view grooming as being something feminine, and that's not true at all. Grooming is life. Being well-groomed will help you feel more confident while also taking care of yourself. We only get one body so it's important to cherish it and treat it well. Getting haircuts and shaving or trimming your beard can help you develop your facial presence. I'm known for having a clean-shaven head and an impeccable beard. I groom my beard thoroughly, I use beard shampoo, beard conditioner, beard balm, and a beard serum. Trimming, brushing, and combing also help maintain the shape I want. Don't be afraid to invest in some

quality products to up your grooming game; grooming is good, trust me.

11. Last but not least, have passion and ambition. As a gentleman in the modern world, you should always have the ambition to improve and the passion to balance it. A wise man once said, "If a man stands for nothing, then he will fall for anything." Have ambition, stand for something, and have passion to back it up. It's okay to believe that black lives matter and in equality for all and women's rights. Be passionate and have ambition to change the world for our future generations – doing so doesn't make you any less of a man. It makes you a gentleman. The kind of gentleman the world needs right now, more than ever!

Black, bald and beautiful as ever.

Manners, style and body confidence is the formula for the sauce. #BauceWithSauce

I put the win in wingtips, baby.

Chapter 3

Loving Yourself

"If you can't love yourself, then you can't love nobody."

– Grandma

My grandma once told me that if you can't love yourself, then you can't love anyone else. I didn't understand this when I was younger, but now as an adult, I understand it with emphasis. You see, it's hard for people to always see the negative in themselves while trying to see the positives in another person. Love is "uncondishy" –especially self-love. Your body is going to change, your opinion about certain topics will change, and most importantly the people around you will change. You are constantly evolving while becoming a better person and dealing with different circumstances in your life. So it only makes sense to love yourself through all these changes in your life. I would be lying to you if I said my body looks the same now as it did when I was in high school – shit, it doesn't even look the same as last year. But that's okay, I love my body and what it has done for me.

As a man, I have suffered from body image insecurities due to media perceptions and ideas of male beauty. Men are held to unrealistic body standards that can alter the way they feel about their bodies. Women go through it just as much, if not more, the only difference is that women have worked to have various body types shown in fashion ads and are able to be vocal about the media's perception of beauty. One of the worst things someone can do is to silence and suppress someone's feelings. The societal standard of

masculinity has silenced men into not being vocal about
their emotional issues, especially body image. So many men
feel the need to look a certain way in order to be treated well
by others. I can relate to the feeling of, "Well, if I had tight
abs and a ripped chest, then people would like me more,
and I would get more interest from people" – this mentality
haunts many men! I have been on the journey to loving
myself for quite some time now, and it's not easy, but I can
tell you this....if you haven't found your worth, now is the
time to do so!! You're one of a kind, and here's my guide to
helping you love yourself.

I have suffered from depression and anxiety in the past, that
shit is real and can get the best of you. Surround yourself
with positive people!! Surround yourself with people who
have such positive vibes that it's hard to not be happy
when around them. Look for people who compliment you,
give you great advice, always build you up, and love you
"uncondishy". Find your self-worth by knowing that no
other person in the world is like you; you're an original,
made one-of-one, and can't be replaced. That's what makes
you unique and special in this world. I for one can tell you
about many times when I was feeling insecure and down on
myself...but one in particular stands out.

My best friend Adam came into town (Columbia, SC) to visit
me and my family. We had some time to catch up on each
other's lives and do some shopping. While we were in the
mall browsing and reminiscing about fun times in college,
we walked past Express. Adam loves Express and has the
perfect build for their clothing, and although I didn't have

the same body type, I had owned some shirts from Express in the past and they had fit perfectly. I had my eye on this Nantucket red blazer...man, it was the most amazing thing I had seen in a while. They had one left, and it was a 44 regular (which was my size at the time), so I went to try it on – but that shit barely went past my elbows!

While I was clearly struggling in the attempt to get this thing over my shoulders and making all kinds of shoulder and arm movements, a sales lady came over and asked if I needed assistance. She attempted to help get the rest of the jacket over my shoulders, but it wasn't going anywhere. She said, "Okay, your arms are just way TOO big. This isn't going to work," and she was right. Unfortunately it didn't fit me, so I did what any other person would do and asked for a larger size. She then informed me that this was the largest size they carried. Clearly I had a puzzled look on my face, because she had just told me that I was basically "TOO big" to fit in that size, and was now telling me that they didn't make a size 46 or 48. She wasn't the most pleasant person either.

I asked her if she could look it up and see if they had a 46 or 48 in another store. She of course said "yes" with *such* an amazing smile and positive attitude (I'm being very sarcastic right now. She was horrible.) She lets me know that was indeed the largest size they carried in the jacket and suggested that I could possibly get one custom made to fit me. Adam was only able to witness a small part of these moments because he was browsing around looking for his own clothing. After he checked out, I told him what had happened, and he was pissed to say the least. He wanted to go back in there and return everything he'd just bought. I convinced him not to, but that's what true friends do, they ride or die. He felt in his heart that if a store treated people that way, then they didn't deserve his business. I must admit I felt pretty down after that terrible shopping experience; in fact, so down that I wanted to talk to someone about it! I wanted to go on my Facebook and lash out against them for not carrying my size as well as providing such horrible customer service. Although I spoke to my wife about my frustration, I had trouble trying to express it on social media. It then dawned on me that men aren't supposed to feel this way; men aren't supposed to feel insecure about their bodies and are perceived to have this "tough guy" image consisting of a "no one can hurt me" type of mentality. It's not true at all. I was hurt...I felt insecure, low, and not good enough.

Days went by and it was still on my mind; for some reason, I just couldn't shake it off. I began exploring why men feel the need to remain silent about problems like body image. I immediately discovered that it's solely based on the societal standard of masculinity. For as long as we can remember, society has given us rules on how men and women should act and feel. Men shouldn't be emotional, but women are supposed to be emotional. I am a man who has emotions, and I wanted to have a voice to express how I really feel... so I created a space to have that voice. I came up with this crazy idea to start a body positive men's fashion blog! I had the idea but had no clue about where to start, what to call it, or anything like that. My wife loved the idea (she supports everything I do because she loves me and believes in me), and asked me different questions about it, but I had no answers. I just knew I wanted to start it and help more men feel confident in their own skin.

When you look through magazines and fashion ads, you see the media's definition of the standard for "ideal male beauty". I wanted to provide an alternative view to what we are used to seeing in those ads by showing that an "average" looking guy can look just as cool in clothes as most of the slim fit models that we see on just about every other fashion site. By "average", I mean that a balding, 5 foot 9, 240 pound black guy can look just as fly or even better in the same clothing. While I was lying in bed one night, it hit me like a flash!! Notoriously Dapper! I woke up my wife in my excitement and asked her what she thought. She agreed that the name was PERFECT. I bought the domain for 99 cents, and the rest is history. My wife and I took outfit pictures daily, and I would post them to my blog and Instagram for people to view, like, and share.

It wasn't always sunshine and rainbows though, there was a dark period. I remember when I first started posting about loving yourself and male body positivity, people would reach out with such negativity. I would get messages like, "If you're so insecure, then hit some effing weights;" "Don't be mad because you're too lazy to get abs;" and my all-time favorite, "You're fat and mad 'cause people that look better than you get attention." These types of messages were from internet trolls. Did it bother me? Yes, of course it did. I would be lying if I told you it didn't, some of the things they said hurt me because I had no other support at the time other than my family. I wasn't a part of the "body positive" community yet; it was mostly women fighting vocally for their right to be accepted as they are. There were plenty of days where I wanted to stop blogging. I didn't see a point of just being online to get bullied by random people I didn't know.

But something happened...something awesome happened. I reached out to Tess Holliday, yeah, that's right, *the* Tess Holliday (the badass plus-size model that kills the internet with her fabulous photos). I asked her about male body image and what she thought about what I was doing at the time, which was advocating for male body positivity. She responded! Not only did she respond, she was excited about what I was doing and gave me excellent advice. This made me feel so great about myself and the message I was promoting. After getting so much online hate from folks and so little love, I got the nod from the queen herself. We spoke a few times after that, and she offered to make me the first and only male member of @effyourbeautystandards, an Instagram page Tess had started to give a middle finger to society's standards and help promote self-love for everyone. Of course I immediately said yes, the thought of not only being accepted in this community but being a part of an Instagram that had helped to start this conversation was amazing. Days passed, and then it was official – after nearly two-plus years of blogging about male body image, I was the newest member of Eff Your Beauty Standards, and the response from the public was jaw-dropping.

People had been waiting for a male to become a part of this movement for quite some time; needless to say, I was happy to help make that possible. The media's unrealistic body images of men and the silencing men often face when dealing with feelings about those images became more clear to people as I discussed them. I have seven of the most body positive badass women in the community in my corner helping me promote a male perspective on positive body image! Creating my blog helped me grow to love myself for who I was and the body I have. I don't have tight abs; I have stretch marks, a receding hairline, and flat feet, and I often stutter over my words, but I'm beautiful the way I am. Surrounding myself with positive people like Tess, Natalie, Harnaam, Aarti, Alison, Rainbow, and Katie (the whole @ effyourbeautystandards gang) made this journey to self-love and acceptance simply marvelous. Meeting people who share the same struggles and emotional fights is inspiring, because you know if they can persevere, then so can you. It makes you strong.

Haters are everywhere, they will find any and everything to hate about someone – that's what they do. Ignore the haters, do what you want, and wear what makes you feel confident. It's okay to get upset by what some people say about you or to you, you're human and you have feelings….that's natural. We can't let it keep us from the greatness in our lives, we have to maintain our composure and understand that you can't change nor give up because someone doesn't like the way you look.

Clothing can change a person's mindset – it can make you feel like you are on top of the world. It can alter the way we handle situations like an interview, for instance. When a man puts on a well-fitted suit, shirt, and tie with some dress shoes, he feels nearly invincible. Stepping into that interview is like Superman stepping out to save the world, you're confident and feel strong...nothing can hold you back from your path of greatness. Wearing clothing that exudes confidence can help you feel more confident about yourself. Clothing may have sizes, but style does not...style has no size. Always remember that! Write it down, take a picture... .I don't care. Just remember it. Anyone of any size can have style, style is the way we show our personality through clothing. We speak to the world about who we are and what we represent by our style. I often compare style to art, our bodies are the naked blank canvas that has nothing but an idea attached to it. The artistic medium is our clothing, from the colors and the patterns to the shoes and the accessories. These, along with our vision, make our masterpiece complete. When we create art, we want to create an image that depicts a mood, a certain feeling, or even an art style (impressionism, pop art, renaissance, etc.), and we do the same with clothing. The way we put certain colors and patterns together can represent that mood, feeling, or style. We create masterpieces daily, and most of us don't even know it. We create walking, talking forms of art by simply getting dressed for the day.

Style is powerful, because it empowers us to be ourselves and have our own identity in this world; it's simple, yet so visually complex. I strongly suggest all men dress well to feel more confident. I mean, if compliments from strangers don't help you feel good about yourself, then we need to start back at square one. A woman once said, "A well-tailored suit is to women what lingerie is to men." Just think about that for a second. Women view men as being sexy when they are dressed up and look, well....Notoriously Dapper. (See what I did there?) Never underestimate the power of clothing. Style can give you enough confidence to help you on this journey of self-love and acceptance, just take it one day at a time.

5 Tips to Help Jump-Start your Self-Love

1. Find something you are confident in. For my own part, I have always been confident in my ability to have style. I found a lot of my confidence through clothes and continue to love myself through my own personal style. Wear what makes you comfortable and happy. Remember, clothing has sizes, but style does not!

2. Look in the mirror and own who you are. Knowing that your body is good enough the way it is. You are 100% original, you cannot be duplicated, and that's what makes you beautiful.

3. Surround yourself with positive people. On this journey to self-love you will have some moments when you don't feel 100% confident, and that's

okay. We all have good and bad body days, but it is important to get that positive boost we all need to get out of our funk and move forward in this journey. Positive energy makes this process a lot easier!

4. Don't compare yourself to others. As I mentioned in Tip 2, we are originals, we can't compare ourselves to other people's bodies or lifestyles. Live your best life and do things that make you happy. I often find myself down in the dumps comparing myself to others, so then I have to stop and reevaluate why I am doing this. This person isn't better than me because they have muscled abs or a chiseled chest. I'm just as awesome as anyone else, because I'm me, and being ourselves is the most pure thing we can be.

5. Keep moving forward. The road to body confidence is different for everyone, two people are not going to share the same tale on this path. It may be long, bumpy, and full of dark areas, but someone else's may be the exact opposite, and that's okay. Just keep loving you, wear what makes you feel happy, have positive people in your corner, and DON'T COMPARE YOURSELF TO OTHERS!

Skies out, thighs out!

Soaking up the sun in my white denim. #StyleHasNoSize

Love yourself before you love anybody else!!

Chapter 4

Benefits of Being Body Confident

"Don't you know your imperfections is a wonderful blessing."

– Kendrick Lamar

A mind is a terrible thing to waste; but many forget a body is a terrible thing to shame. Body shaming is what the media often does to make us feed into their perception of beauty. Shaming someone, especially about his or her body, is never acceptable for any reason. Body shaming comes in all different forms, from subtle hints to having someone straight up tell you your body isn't good enough. For some that can be hard to ignore. Even the most confident person in the world has bad body days and can feel unconfident on certain days for whatever reason. You know what I'm talking about, those days where you feel like you have nothing to wear (because you just don't feel good in anything you put on).

It's not just a girl problem, ladies – many guys go through this, we just don't vocalize it. You could say the societal standard of men has in some way shamed men into thinking that these "feelings" aren't real. They are real, very real in fact, so real that I'm writing about it right now! It's important to become body confident not only for yourself but for others. We all have been around that "negative Nancy" type of person that just seems to hate everything about anything. A big benefit to being body confident is that you tend to be less negative to yourself and others – we can all agree that's always a positive change.

Having confidence in your body and who you are will help you have prosperous relationships. Whether it be a friendship or a romantic relationship, self-confidence will lead you to improve those connections with positivity. Listen, no one wants to date or be friends with someone who always tears themselves down. We all have known that one person who can never find anything positive in how they look, feel, or dress. That honestly can put a strain on your relationships, especially ones where the other person is positive and tries to lift you up. It makes them feel like there is nothing they can do or say that is good enough to make you feel better about yourself. That alone can be draining for someone; no one wants to be around that individual who just can't seem to take a compliment. You tell them how nice they look, and they respond with something negative like, 'I wish I had done this or that to my hair, by the way I hate my hair and blah blah blah.' Those negative responses can quickly change someone's mood and how they feel about you. I know there are people in the world who don't have much self-confidence, but you need to find the strength to accept compliments even at your worst moments.

Honestly, if someone gives you a compliment, chances are they are being 100% honest with you about how they feel. You need to take that and apply it to your confidence bank. "A confidence bank? What the hell is that?" you may ask. Well, it is a bank of confidence that lives in your heart and soul. Some of us have a lot in our bank, some have little to nothing, and some are in debt. It doesn't matter where you are now, it only matters about getting your confidence bank full enough for you to reap the benefits. Truth be told,

I never thought I had a good smile until people told me what a beautiful smile I had. I started to take notice and view my smile in more positive light. This positive feedback started to build up some serious change in my confidence bank, and I started to smile more often. When I reached a certain level in my confidence bank, it was then time for me to cash out and reap the benefits of that confidence level, which were smiling and being more appreciative of others' compliments!

When you have positive vibes, you radiate them to others. As Clemson University's Coach Dabo Swinney would say, "Let the light inside of you shine brighter than the light that's shining on you". Now, I'm a strong Gamecocks supporter, I bleed garnet and black all day every day, but even I can get behind that. That kind of positive attitude led Clemson to accomplish the greatest achievement in college football, a national championship win over the undefeated Alabama Crimson Tide. You see, if Dabo had been a "negative Nancy" and hadn't built his team up, they could have lost that game. They didn't lose because they had love, love for themselves, love for their bodies, love for the game, and most importantly, love for one another. Think of how many things you could do with some body confidence...the kind of confidence that helps a 300-pound lineman do the splits on national television after winning a championship (Clemson again, dammit!) If that's not confidence, then I don't know what is. We all come in different shapes, colors, and sizes. We are all built for greatness; you just have to believe it.

Believing can be difficult sometimes, you see; they say that seeing isn't believing, but that believing is seeing. As a black man, seeing the way men of color are portrayed in the media and society can hinder our self-confidence and self-worth. Men aren't supposed to be emotional in any way, and if we are, we are perceived as being weak. We are supposed to be confident, strong, and tough in every way. How can you be body confident if your body isn't seen as mattering as much as other bodies? How can you feel comfortable in your own skin when you are always profiled because of your skin? How can you love yourself when the media puts so much hate and fear on the idea of a black man? Everyone's body confidence journey is different, though they are all beautiful.

My journey to being a body confident black man has not been an easy one. I view my clothes as both my savior and my armor. Style has helped me become more confident in life while also helping me be viewed as less of a threat to society. I feel confident in what I choose to wear, and when I style an outfit, I feel invincible – it helps me to exude body confidence. It's sad that we live in a world where you're more valued in a suit than you are in a hoodie. Whether I'm in a blazer or hoodie, I am still the same confident positive individual that I was when I got dressed. I can honestly say that my confidence took a hit when I watched numerous news outlets reporting unarmed black men being gunned down. It just happened one after the other, and it's hard to worry about body confidence when your body doesn't matter. It's hard to feel comfortable in your own skin when you may be gunned down because of your skin. Men suffer from fear, anxiety, and depression; they are real emotions and should not be ignored. We can never forget that men suffer from these issues. Giving them an outlet to speak about their insecurities and emotions will help breed brave men for future generations. We all deserve to feel safe, loved, and celebrated, not feared, hated, and ignored.

I take 10 mg of Prozac daily, and it helps me with my daily worries and anxiety. It may have taken me more than 15 years to realize I have anxiety issues, but you know what they say, better late than never. I felt ashamed when I was diagnosed with anxiety; I was concerned I was going to be viewed as being weak. I didn't realize that people could suffer from such a thing and how it can be literally crippling to your life. I have learned to love myself through being true to who I am. I have a wonderful support system of friends and family who embrace me for the original person I am. I have learned through years of personal experience how to care for my mental and physical health. My style is me, and I am style. I think it's vital to wear what makes you feel happy and surround yourself with positive energy. It makes the bad body days good and the good body days better. Everyone has a struggle we don't know about, so always be nice to people, even when they are being negative towards you. Kindness can change the world – when you are kind to yourself and others, you can truly make this world a better place. It's easier to be caring to others when you care for yourself. We often forget about ourselves in this busy life we live. Be sure to care for yourself, take a mental health day from work and do something that makes you happy.

Go to the beach in the bathing suit you love, and know that your body is a beach body. Oftentimes we have this false expectation of what a "beach body" looks like. With magazine covers saying things like, "Get your body beach ready with this new diet," it's hard to understand that your body is *already* beach ready. Let me tell you the easiest way to get your body beach ready. Simply take your ass to a beach in whatever attire makes you feel comfortable! I can recall MANY times I have felt self-conscious about my body while going to the beach. I would wear long pants and shirts to the beach while everyone else was enjoying themselves freely in their bathing suits. I wanted to hide my stretch marks, my legs, and the fat on my belly. I was missing out on having a good time with my friends and family when going to the beach or pool. I used to hate taking off my shirt and felt so uncomfortable in a bathing suit, but then I realized it was all mental. As I got older, I became more body confident. I started to realize that most people don't go to the beach to body shame others, unless they're just terrible human beings. It's usually only on the internet and in magazines where you have people trying to body shame an individual. People go to the beach to have fun, not to engage in body shaming. It wasn't till my junior year of college that I started to be comfortable shirtless in my bathing suit, and now I'm modeling shirtless for a company that sells bathing suits...crazy, right? It's funny how things work out. If I hadn't become body confident, then I would have missed the opportunity to do that modeling job with Chubbies Shorts.

Lack of confidence can lead you to miss opportunities! Including opportunities that could change your life for the better, such as modeling for Chubbies Shorts, which has changed my life in many ways. It has helped me on my road to body acceptance in the fashion industry and in my everyday life. When I became body confident enough to wear a bathing suit shirtless, especially on camera, it lifted up the 100 pound weight that was holding me back from pursuing my passion for fashion. I would have never had the courage to enter that man-modeling contest. Yes, that's right, I became a model by winning a contest. Chubbies Shorts (a brand based out of San Francisco, California, that sells awesome 80's style shorts with a 5.5 inch inseam) held an online contest to find their next male models. I saw the ad one day scrolling through the web, so I decided to fill out an online application. Hell, I had nothing to lose, so I shared it on my social media outlets and somehow made it to the top 20!

My body type is not represented in fashion ads, so naturally I wanted to change that, now that I had the confidence enough to put myself out there. No matter how much negativity I received, I was determined to make this happen for myself and other men who suffer from body insecurities. I was sick of being told I could never model because I was too short, too big, or my personal favorite, the passive-aggressive "You just don't fit what we're looking for right now" – which really meant, "We aren't looking for someone of your size or race, so move on, sir." I was told NO hundreds of times by agencies, but finally something gave. I encouraged my following to vote for me, and they did. They came through with all the love and positive vibes; many people wanted to see me win, so they made it happen. I won the male model contest based on public voting and officially became a model for Chubbies Shorts!

This is a company that helped me feel more confident in shorts through their advertising. Before I found out about them, I was wearing those long-ass baggy shorts during the summer, but the only problem was that I have pretty big thighs, so big that they touch when I stand or walk (which I'm totally okay with) – as some people say, "my thighs are so sexy they can't stop touching each other." For me personally, one of the most uncomfortable things is wearing a pair of shorts that ride up in your crotch area, and that's what would happen when I wore the baggy shorts. I would have to constantly stop to readjust myself while walking. When I bought my first pair of Chubbies, it was a relief, because I had found a pair of stylish shorts that fit my limitations – and best of all, they didn't ride up. The 5.5 inch inseam helps your thighs breathe while staying cool during the hot weather. I would never have thought in a million years that I would be a model for them...it just goes to show that there is a plan for all of us. The road to it may be bumpy and seem unstable, but you have to believe in yourself and trust the process. What is meant to be, will be, no matter how many obstacles you hit along your way.

Don't be afraid to show the world that you love yourself. You're one of a kind, and no one in the world is like you at all. Truth be told, when you have this kind of confidence it's easier to be more comfortable with yourself. Being comfortable with who you are is a HUGE help towards being body confident, you will be able to rock that bathing suit you were scared to put on before. Certain insecurities will be transformed into affirmations, like how you think you look in your outfit, how you feel when approaching a stranger to converse, or even simply going out with a group of friends. Others will see how comfortable you are with your body image, and it will radiate an aura of confidence that will be contagious to others. This will attract more positive people in your life and reassure you that the path you are on is the right one. Continue to spread love and awareness to your friend, boyfriend, husband, brother, dad, uncle, and nephew.

The Benefits of Being Body Confident

- Improved relationships and friendships with others.
- The ability to take advantage of important opportunities.
- Rocking that beach body will be amazing.
- A contagious aura that radiates positivity to others.
- Finding out that you are good enough the way you are.
- Insecurities will become affirmations.
- Finding the positives in yourself and others.
- Attract more positive people in your life.
- Be able to own who you are.

Body confidence is for EVERYONE. Every age, size, race, and gender!

Wanna know how to get a beach body?! It's simple, have a body and take yo ass to the beach!
#BeYouBeConfident

Showing something natural like a back with some stretch marks! #TigerStripes

Dapperly dressed down

Chapter 5

Choosing to Be Great

"Quitting isn't an option, I did not raise any quitters. As a black male in America you have to be great. There is no other option. The world doesn't love you like I do."

—Mom

We all want to be great at what we do, but most people don't know the hours of work, the sacrifices, and the quantity of failures that are associated with greatness. Greatness isn't given; it is earned, and it is a choice to earn it. When I speak of being great, I'm not talking about being the best at something. Being the best is never going to happen, because someone will always be better in a sense. Greatness is internal and can only be sought by you for you.

I started pop lock dancing around the 9th grade. It was a cool dance that I saw these upperclassmen doing at lunch one day, and I was amazed by their control of their bodies and movements. It didn't look real, but it was. I was completely driven and wanted to learn how to do it. I could already dance a little bit, so I decided to show them some moves. They were impressed with how I got down. I began to attend little pop lock/breakdance competitions every now and then. I was amazed by how much talent was there. Dancers came from all over the place ready to give it their all. Well, time went by and it was my turn to battle...this dancer was named Baby Doc, and man, was he good. He killed me, completely destroyed me in every way possible in that dance battle.

I remember leaving the competition thinking, how did I lose so badly? I felt embarrassed and ashamed to even call myself a dancer. I decided to get better by practicing more to a variety of music. I would also work out to get my endurance up. I was determined to not let that happen to me again. So after months of practice and hard work, I decided to go back to another dance competition. I made it to the fourth round and was feeling great about myself. It was my turn to go against one of the best dancers in Charlotte. The lights dimmed, and the music started pumping! I looked at my opponent as we both paced back and forth, waiting for someone to make the first move to start the battle. I saw his shoulders start moving, and he began to step to the dance floor, calling me out with every single move imaginable. He was amazing and had great rhythm, but now it was my turn. I was super nervous and just kept thinking, what if I suck? I finally shook off the mental negativity and started dancing, arm waving, doing the robot and all kinds of new footwork. I for sure felt confident about making it to the semifinals. When it was time for the judges to decide who won, I was not chosen.... and pure heartbreak hit me. I had come so far and done so well, but wasn't great enough to make it to the semifinals.

I felt discouraged and really didn't want to attend any more dance battles. I laid low for a while and didn't really dance much. Then I went out with some friends one night, and the music was just too good for me not to dance, so I did. I began moving and grooving in a new way unlike anything I had ever done before. I felt good, confident, and reaffirmed that I could be a dance champion in Charlotte.

I attended little battles here and there to build up my spirit and dance moves. Two years later, I showed up to the annual dance battle at the breakfast club in Charlotte, NC. I remember it like it was yesterday. I walked in after nearly two years of being away from the Charlotte dance scene. It was an 80's style dance club, so people were always dressed super 80's fresh, rocking everything from Adidas jumpsuits to Jane Fonda-inspired Jazzercise outfits. It was always a great time. As I started seeing familiar faces and catching up with old dance friends, I realized I needed to sign up to battle before the sign up time closed. There's a part where you have to fill out your dance name (what you want to be called when they introduce you); my old dance name had been "Smoothie", but I changed it right then and there to "Nugget". I wanted a new dance identity to reflect the new and better dancer I had become. Of course I was the underdog during this competition. I mean, I had been completely absent from the Charlotte dance scene for almost two years! There were a lot of new faces and young upcoming dancers who were super dope. Although I was surrounded by all this new energy, I was confident; I was ready to give it my all and be great. I made it through the first, second, and third rounds.

The judges took the winner from each round and had the three of us compete in a three-way battle. This was my first time ever being a part of a three-way battle. I started to get nervous. I had made it to the final round, and my nerves were getting the best of me. We had a 20-minute intermission for dancers to get drinks, socialize, and mentally prepare for the three-way battle. I went to the bathroom and stared at myself in the mirror, splashed water on my face, and asked myself if I was ready. I had trained so hard for this moment, and I didn't want to blow it because of my nerves. I went back out there to get prepared for this battle; I talked to one of my dance friends, Archie, who was telling me how good I had gotten over the years and that I had nothing to worry about, because I was great. Sometimes we all need a little bit of a boost to send us above and beyond, and he gave me that boost.

The lights dimmed and the MC came on over the speakers. He called for everyone to clear the dance floor. It was show time; it was now or never. He called out my name last, and as I was making my way through the crowd to get to the dance floor, I saw my friends Alan, Devon, and Greg giving me a thumbs-up. We stood in a triangle on the dance floor waiting for the music to drop. Those seconds seemed like minutes going by; finally, the music dropped and one of the dancers started moving into the center of the dance floor, pointing at me (calling me out). I stepped up to accept his challenge. He signaled for me to go back to my spot and started dancing. He was good, he used his moves to manipulate the beat, and his body control was out of this world, to say the least. His time ended, and the second dancer started dancing, calling me out with every move he made (by imitating some of the previous moves I had done).

Then it was my turn, as the music continued to play, I heard the bass go BOOM, BOOM, BOOM, and I started to move my hands, feeling the beat. I stepped out to the floor, and something happened. I danced like I had never danced before. Every move caused the crowd to roar louder and louder, I was feeling myself, to say the least – calling out each dancer as I was popping, waving, and gliding through the music. It was time for the judges to decide the winner of the battle; the MC came to the microphone and congratulated us on an entertaining battle night. Then he called on the judges to choose the winner. I was sweating profusely…and the MC said, "Judges, on the count of three, point to your winner. One, two…three! They all pointed to me and I fucking lost it, I jumped up and down with joy. It was pure disbelief, but at the same time, I was confident I was going to win because I CHOSE to be great that night. I had the intention of not leaving without a win. It felt good to know my hard work had paid off.

You see, when you work hard, you will eventually reap the benefits. Too many times in this day and age people want instant results with little to no work being put in. That's not the way life works at all! Something that separates people who are successful from people who are not is the ability to try, put in work, persevere, believe in yourself, love the struggle, and embrace the hustle. You will fail, failure is inevitable…don't be afraid to fail, without failure, there is no success. Great people try more than once, and they don't give up after the first, second, or even third try. They continue to put in work and persevere through failure and those difficult moments. Getting results is not easy, I mean imagine if Alexander Bell had given up the first time he tried to invent the telephone, or if I had given up on my first time trying to buy Yeezy's from the Adidas site (getting to success took so many L's). Eventually I got a W (a win) on the Yeezy 350 V2 "Oreo" Colorway, which was a good day. Persevere through the negativity and L's while believing in yourself, because eventually you will get that W.

Life is hard, it's that simple. Nothing will be given to you, nor will it be easy for you to earn it. Obstacles are a part of the path to success; it's bumpy, there are hills, dark spots, and plenty of pitfalls that will take the best out of you and make you want to give up. They can make you question why you even started on the path in the first place. Never look back; if you do, only look back to see how far you've come, what obstacles you've defeated, and how much negativity you've ignored. On the path to being great, you will need a good support system. Trust me, those downfall moments will get you in a dark place, especially when they all arrive at once. You know that day where you're late to work, your car has a flat tire, your coffee order was messed up, and it just seems like nothing can go right for you. Those days can get the best of you and put you in a place that can alter your mood entirely. But having some good support will get you through those tough times, having positive people to help you see the light in a situation when you only can see the darkness. They guide you to the light with their positive uplifting words of encouragement and motivate you to continue down that path of success.

Love the struggle, without it we have no need to appreciate the hustle. The hustles of work, school, life in general, or parenting are full of great, good, and bad moments, moments that will motivate you to embrace the hustle you have started. Being a plus-size male model is a struggle for sure. We men don't have a place yet in the fashion industry, though everywhere there are now size diversity ads that embrace a woman's body for the beauty of what it is. I have been on this path to body positivity for a while; it is filled with daily struggles, but you appreciate those good body days when you have bad body days.

You can't appreciate the good without the bad, that's just life. We love to forget about the positives in our life when negativity strikes. We tend to dwell too much on what is going wrong rather than what is going right. My dad always told me you judge someone's character by how they perform during hard times. He would say to me, "It's easy to be in a good mood when everything is going right, when it's all sunshine and rainbows, but life isn't all like that. There are plenty of storms, and how you weather through those storms says a lot more about your character than how you weather sunshine." He's right. You have to choose to be great! You have to choose to persevere through those tough times and continue to put in that hard work to get the results you want in this life. NO EXCUSES! Anybody can be anything at any moment, you just have to believe in yourself. Keep smiling and moving forward, this life is full of opportunities for you to be great. The road to greatness is waiting for you, just remember these words.

10 Characteristics You Will Need to Be Great:

1. You will need perseverance, the ability to accomplish something despite how difficult or impossible it may seem. Once upon a time, we were all babies and couldn't walk, talk, write, or read. We had to work to learn how to do such things. When you started your first steps as a child, you weren't worried about how many times you fell and failed. You got back up and tried again until you began to walk. As adults, it's easy for us to just say, "Naw, I can't do it. I give up." But we have to always think back to when we were kids ourselves and remember the perseverance we showed when attempting to walk, talk, write, and read. It wasn't easy, and it takes some longer than others, but as long as you get to your goal it doesn't matter what the road ahead entails. Stay with it!

2. Responsibility is major when choosing to be great. You need to rely on your own ability to make your way. Yes, it's okay to accept help along the way and take good advice. But ultimately you decide to be great, you choose whether or not you're going to wake up at 5 a.m. to practice those jump shots in order to be a better basketball player. When you don't succeed the first time, it's okay, but make sure to take responsibility for your part and find ways to improve. Being responsible will not only help you on your road to success but will help you with life's daily obstacles as well.

3. Motivation is the mental motor behind all your pursuits. Having self-motivation will help you accomplish anything you want in this life. Find things to help motivate you like inspiring videos, words, or even role models in the field you are trying to pursue. View someone else's success as motivation, not with jealousy; be happy for that person's accomplishments and seek to reach their level or go even further. Every area of greatness has an example of how to become great! Follow the lead of the greats and be motivated to become greater.

4. Have passion for what you are pursuing. It's easy to lose motivation when you are not passionate about what you are pursuing. Don't pursue being great at something for the sake of others, that's an easy way to get caught in a miserable career field. Do it for yourself! Follow your heart and pursue what makes you happy; if you want to be a painter, do it, if you want to be a cobbler, do it, if you want to be a mailman, do it, and if you want to be a farmer, just do it. Whatever you want to be, just be it and be happy. People put too much emphasis on money, but money cannot buy you happiness. My mom told me when I was in college, "Make sure you do what you love, and it will never feel like work." I have always had the passion for fashion, ALWAYS. I have always wanted to inspire others to be better, dress better, and act better. So, I decided to follow my heart and create Notoriously Dapper! I can honestly say none of this feels like "work" – it's a passion, so it just feels

natural, like I was made to do this. You will feel the same if you just follow your heart and have passion for what you are pursuing!

5. Stay focused, don't let distractions get in your way to greatness. Distractions come in all different forms: humans, depression, anxiety, etc. It's important to work through those distractions and not let them get in the way of your path to success. If you have people in your life who are holding you back and distracting you from your goal, then let them go. Sometimes we have to put things in the past to move forward. The fewer distractions you have, the more focused you can be on what you want to accomplish. If your goal is to graduate from high school and you're hanging around the "wrong crowd" of people, then you may have to let them go in order to accomplish that goal of graduating. It's okay to be selfish if you are trying to become better for yourself and others. It's simple: more focus, less distraction.

6. Failure is inevitable, own and embrace it. We are all going to fail and feel as if we can't accomplish our goal because of it. Little do people know, failure is great. Without failure, you wouldn't have traits like motivation or perseverance. Failure is a necessity when trying to succeed. Embracing failure will help you persevere and stay motivated. You may not get that "dream job" the first, second, or third time, but you may get it the sixth time. Everything has a time, remember, just because it's not right now doesn't mean it's never.

7. Be open to advice and knowledge from others. Sometimes it may be difficult to hear the truth, but the truth will set you free. Honest good advice is one of the best things you can receive on this road to greatness. The advice I'm giving you right now will help you accomplish those goals! Don't close this book or close out a friend or family member for trying to give you advice. Chances are if they mean well, their advice will help you a lot more than hurt you.

8. Be enthusiastic about your journey to greatness. If you're following your passion, then you should have no reason not to be happy about the pursuit. Yes, it will be a rough and bumpy road, but having enthusiasm will make it a lot more enjoyable. Smile, laugh, and be lighthearted during your pursuit of greatness. You never know what kind of obstacles will be thrown in your way, but a little enthusiasm will set you apart from others on the same journey.

9. One of the biggest characteristics you will need to have is the ability to sacrifice. Time is the most precious possession we have. Sacrificing time with your family and friends can sometimes be necessary to reach the goal you seek. For example, if your goal is to be a scientist, there is a certain number of lab hours you will need plus a certain amount of research and training. Those lab hours may force you to sacrifice time at a party, dinner, or get-together. Make sure you balance your sacrifices, though. You will have to make some sacrifices to become great, but don't over-sacrifice. Weigh the importance of each situation, for

example, don't miss your best friend's wedding or your parent's birthday party because of your pursuit of greatness. Don't ruin relationships on your journey – remember, some things can be postponed and some things can't. Choose your sacrifices wisely!

10. Love the hustle and work the struggle. What does that mean? Well, it means love that journey to greatness and everything it entails while working through your struggles. I am quite the minority in the fashion industry because of my size and race. I worked through that struggle of being told, "No, you're too big to model" – if everything was easy to obtain, then we would all do it. What separates me from anyone else in this industry is that I thrive on being told no. That means when I accomplish it, I have proved you wrong. I love when people say, "That's impossible, it's never been done before." Good! That means I will be the first to do it. I was one of the first body positive activists for men, and I didn't let any distraction stop me from what I wanted to pursue. I felt confident through my style and wanted to spread that same confidence to other men. Now Notoriously Dapper has become a place for men of all sizes to gain confidence and style advice. The hustle is hard, the struggle is real – but the DREAM is free, GO FOR IT!

When you look good, you feel good. When you feel good, you do good. When you do good, you smile good!

In my Mr. Clean stance ready for warm weather

Damnnnnnnn Dapper, back at it again with the fresh threadsssss!

I don't strip, baby, I stripe. #PunnyGuy

Chapter 6

The Bro Code

"I ride for my guys, that's the bro code."

– Young M.A.

Friends, how many of us have them? Friends, they are the people we can depend on. We all deserve someone we can depend on and talk to. Friends help us stay sane, laugh, enjoy boring moments, and guide us in the right direction. We all need good friends, the kind who will tell you when you're being stupid while giving you brutally honest advice. Those kind of friends help build character and also guide you to make the right decisions to be successful in life. I can honestly say I wouldn't be the man I am today if it wasn't for good friends. I believe people are sent into our life for a season or for a reason. Some friends we have are temporary, but they are still friends. You may only be friends with them because of a circumstance, like a classmate, roommate, or your friend's friend. People come into our lives to help us or open our eyes to something new, good or bad. Being aware will help you notice why your friend is there for you.

Bromance is a term for a male companionship that is deeply rooted in emotion, the past, and a shared personal history. So, how do you know if you have a good bromance? Well my friends Adam, Alan, and Devon are pretty good examples of good male companionship. When I transferred to the University of South Carolina, I didn't have any friends there besides my girlfriend at the time. My random roommate Taylor was a cool guy, and he introduced me to Alan and

Adam. Alan is from Atlanta, and he loved kart racing. Adam was this cool Jewish guy who roomed on our hall and made AMAZING hip-hop beats on his laptop. Alan, Adam, Taylor, and I would always go out for power hour and try to pick up girls with "collegiate swagger". Some nights we were successful, but what we built that semester was a strong foundation of companionship.

When summer came, we all went back to our home towns and reached out a few times to keep in touch. I ended things with my girlfriend when I transferred that summer and worked on starting a new path for my sophomore year of college. Alan and Adam decided to room together at Bates West, and I chose to live in an apartment-like South Quad dorm room. I was supposed to room with Taylor, but the stars didn't align, and I got put in a dorm room with two USC football players. They were awesome roommates, but we lived separate lives; they were seniors getting ready to graduate in December and move on to the real world. Meanwhile, I was just a sophomore still trying to find my way in the college lifestyle.

South Quad wasn't that far of a walk from Bates West, plus Taylor lived near me in another room. So I was still close to my friends, and we hung out all the time. We would eat lunch and dinner together often and even go out for drinks a few times a week. Adam got us into all the underage drinking spots and also provided liquor with his fake ID. We would have amazing times and conversations both serious and comical; the more we knew about each other, the more we opened up to one another. We told each other about our futures, what we wanted to be, where we wanted to live, and more. We often talked about our relationships at the time and whether we would marry our current girlfriends or possibly keep on as bachelors looking for love and whatnot.

Adam had ended his long-term relationship with his girlfriend since high school and was ready to move on to the single party life. I, on the other hand, had just started a new relationship, and it was blossoming at the time (though it was based off of lies). She didn't know that I would go out, drink, and party till like one or two in the morning. Fast forward, a few months later I was walking into a local bar with my friends and I saw my girlfriend at the time dancing and grinding on this random dude. I double-checked to make sure it was her, and it was – so I blacked out in a drunken rage and attacked the guy like a raging animalistic monster (not cool at all). She was all drunk and was like, "What's the fucking deal, Kelvin?! You're drunk too!" My friends were holding me back and trying to figure out what was going on. So as I was getting counseled by my besties with testes, I noticed her drunkenly crying in a corner with her friends, probably telling them how much of an asshole I was and whatnot, because that's what happens when shit like that goes on.

So my friends convince me to take an "L" for the night and go home. I woke up the next morning to insane text messages – everything from drunken "I hate you's" to loving heartfelt apologies. I decided to respond to her texts and explain why I had lied about not drinking, since she had given me the reason why she had gone out. She'd said it was her roommate's birthday and given me a "we didn't plan to go out, it just happened," type of excuse. Later that day, I met with Alan and Adam for dinner at Russell's house, I was nervous because I hadn't talked to them all day, and I was expecting them to lecture me about my behavior. Instead, when they greeted me, they called me a "raging teddy bear" and made jokes out of it. It was nice to have friends take something so stressful and make light of it. During dinner, Adam mentioned how I had turned into a grizzly bear as I entered the bar, knocking over barstools and people. They made me feel good by making fun of the situation and how ridiculous it was. I knew then that these would be my friends for a very very long time! It's been over ten years, and we are still great friends.

Alan is the kind of friend who helps you get your life in order while telling you to taste a new beer he's discovered at a local brewery. Adam is the guy who listens to the newest hip-hop album with you and gives you his opinion and his interpretation of it. He also loves art and fashion; he's pretty much the "Ivory" version of me. I met Devon through Alan in our sophomore year of college, he and Alan had attended rival high schools in Atlanta. As our sophomore year of college was coming to an end, Adam informed us that he was going to transfer to USC Beaufort so he could be closer to home and work. We knew he had been having a hard time; although we were there for him and tried to help him through his tough times, he knew what was best for him. Alan, Devon, and I decided to room together in an apartment complex off campus. We moved in together at the end of July and we were back together, the three amigos;

the only issue was that we had moved into a four-bedroom apartment thinking Adam was going to join us, so when he decided to move back home, we had to opt for a random potluck roommate, and we had no clue who we were going to get.

On move in day, I met our new potluck roommate Shawn, and he was the exact opposite of how we were. He didn't party, had never consumed alcohol, and barely used foul language (kind of like me in my freshman year). Also, he mentioned that he had never had a black friend before and was excited to live with me! I tell you, the things people say sometimes just make me cringe, while thinking, "Do they know it's not okay to say shit like that?" Anyway, we were roommates, and we had to live together. It was my freshman year all over again, except the roles were reversed – I was Taylor and Shawn was me in my first year. I got Shawn drunk and took him out for the first time; it was almost like a circle of gentlemanly gestures. Everything Taylor had done for me I did for Shawn to make him feel comfortable and to show him I was a good friend. I wanted Shawn to trust me the same way I trusted Taylor! Shawn was quirky and had his moments, like blasting live Christina Aguilera concerts at eight in morning on a fucking Saturday! Word of advice, never do anything involving loud noise around your roommates early in the morning on a weekend, it's not cool. Some people are trying to rest up and cure their hangover and continue their fantasy of having coffee with Kathy Bates.

Let me tell you about the first time I got Shawn drunk along with Alan and Devon. Shawn wanted to go out drinking and dancing, his thing was salsa dancing. He wasn't bad at it, either – he just looked funny showing people how to salsa with no partner in sight. We decided to go to this new club called "Bleu", it was college night and drinks were half off. Before going out, we would always make 'pre-game' preparations by drinking and listening to music to get ready for the night's festivities. Shawn may have had too much to drink before we even left to go clubbing. Anyway, we arrived at the club, and we were too lit! We started in dancing, drinking, and spitting game to beautiful women; needless to say T-Pain was insanely popular at the time, so we were all singing "I'm'a buy you a drank" at the top of our lungs. We danced for a few more songs, then decided to head back to the "513" which was how we referred to our apartment, because our apartment number was 513. Of course we got a taxi back, because drinking and driving is NOT cool in any way, shape or form.

Getting food was a late-night requirement for us after drinking and dancing all night, so we went to get pizza, and Shawn was loving it. He told us how much fun he had and how he wanted to do it again next weekend. When we got back home, he began to throw up everywhere. Mind you, he had never been drunk or had to go through this. He reminded me of myself when Taylor got me drunk for the first time. I was feeling high on life, then I felt terrible with him puking all over the place. I knew this was the world's way of transferring good karma – it was my turn to repay what Taylor had done for me. Shawn kept asking for someone to rub his back while holding his hair back, and I decided to be that friend he needed. I went into the bathroom and held his lack of hair back (he had clearly watched too many Sex and the City episodes) – the funny thing about it was that Shawn didn't have enough hair to hold back at all. So I pretended like I was holding it so he felt like someone was there for him, and yes, I rubbed his hairy back. I then gave him water to hydrate himself and made sure he got to bed safely.

The next day he woke up looking like a train had hit him. We joked with him and said, "No Christina this morning, huh?" He said he didn't want to hear any music for the rest of the weekend. We all burst into laughter because he was so serious, and we knew how much he loved Christina Aguilera! It felt good to pay it forward and show the same compassion someone had shown me in the same circumstance. I tell you, everything happens for a reason! Have you ever needed help and someone helped you, and then a similar situation happened and you feel obligated to help them because you've been in the same situation? That's God's way of testing you and making sure you will return the good karma.

We had more interesting moments throughout our time living together that I will leave alone because they are super embarrassing. Our senior year was approaching, and just like always, we had to discuss our plans for living situations. Alan, Devon, and I decided to stay at the 513 and ride it out until graduation. Shawn moved to another apartment near ours to make room for Devon's best friend Greg to move in.

There was no bad blood with Shawn, but his friends lived around the corner, and they had a room open. Greg really wanted to live with us, so it just worked out, or as I like to say, the stars aligned. Greg ate nothing but ramen noodles and peanut butter sandwiches; he also ran seven to ten miles every day. He would go to sleep as if he was going to bed for the night, but then wake up at like 11 at night and run for hours. Greg was the definition of being your own fucking man, he did what he wanted when he wanted to do it and owned the shit out of it. What I liked most about Greg was his ability to be friendly to everyone and to get along with thugs, preps, frat dudes, and just about any other type of person you can imagine. Greg was the fresh holy water the 513 needed to get through our senior year.

Along with Greg, I met Michael, Clay, and Kevin. Michael was friends with Alan, and Michael's best friend was Michele (aka Meesh). Clay and Kevin were friends with Devon, so we spent a lot of time at their apartment in Olympia Mills. Our senior year was a more sophisticated version of our past years; we drank better beer, didn't go out a lot, and kept to our circle of friends. The best thing about this was Michael; he introduced me to my now-wife Michele (at the time she was just a friend of ours). We would go out and she would bring her girlfriends, so when we were together, we were deep in numbers. It was always a fun time, because sometimes we would just party at the apartment and stay there the entire night, talking and playing drinking games. I loved what our friends had evolved into – we had finally made it to the end of our senior year. It was bittersweet, because we often had talked about our living situation, but it was clear that we had to move on. Devon took a job in Charlotte working for Bank of America, Alan moved to Charlotte as well to work, and Greg decided to pursue his career as a scriptwriter. I had alternative plans because Michele, now my girlfriend, (Michele) was pregnant. I knew I had to take care of our situation and continue to be a supportive partner during this time. I actually still had to do student teaching the next semester and then graduate in December. I had planned on graduating on time, but as my dad says, "If you ever want to hear God laugh at you, tell him your plans."

As our lives took different directions and we went our separate ways, we continued to stay in touch and look out for one another. Thank God for texting and Facebook birthday reminders, otherwise we would be shit out of luck, to say the least. I think the most important thing about building a strong bromance is the ability to find time to chat and check in with your friends. It's important to know when they leave a job, move, or are dating someone new. We are all in serious relationships now; while I'm the only one who is married with kids, I know they are not too far behind me in that area. We often reunite for Carolina football tailgate parties, which is simply amazing – we get to catch up, and my kids get to hang out with their Uncles! I never had a brother, so these guys are the closest thing I will ever have to one. I can honestly say I have four brothers that I can count on for anything. If I am ever in a bad place financially, mentally, or physically, I know they will drop everything and come to my rescue without any questions. Make sure you have friends who help first and ask questions later. If you can't rely on them, then you shouldn't consider them a friend. Friends are reliable, fun, positive, and make you a BETTER person! These guys have shown me true friendship over these past ten years. We have had ups and downs, but what we have built will last forever. Every time we talk, it's like we never skipped a beat, we just pick up where we left off and keep it moving forward.

It's a beautiful thing to have people you can count on for anything at any given moment. When being a friend, remember your role. Your role is to be positive, fun, non-judgmental, and reliable. Make sure they always have your best interests at heart; like Drake says, "I've got fake friends showing fake love to me". You don't want that fake love. You want the real deal, the realness that lets you know when you're being an asshole or when to go ahead and do something, and gives you advice that HELPS you in your life. My friends have never encouraged violence, hostility, or any negative behavior, and that's what you need. Now, that doesn't mean that they wouldn't have my back if something were to happen, because they would. We look out for one another, positivity is always our first thought. I love these guys to death! They threw me one hell of a bachelor party in Atlanta, and I will never speak of what happened that night – because that's against the bro code!

The Bro Code Guidelines

- Be reliable.

- Keep in contact.

- Help one another out.

- Always give honest and constructive advice.

- Never date your friend's ex under any circumstance.

- Be fun.

- Don't judge.

- Make sure your friends complement you and what you represent.

- Don't let religion, race, or political views affect your Bromance.

- Always return the good karma.

- Relive memories while making new ones.

- Be the friend that makes them a better person.

- Encourage them when they are down.

- Know your role as their Bro.

Orange you going to smile?!

Style so cold it snowed in March! #TheraFlu

Chapter 7

The Art of Courtship

"I believe that marriage isn't between a man and woman; but between love and love."

– Frank Ocean

We live in a world where people from anywhere can fall in love with anyone at any time. That is truer today than ever before, with dating apps like Tinder, Match, and EHarmony, it's easy to connect and find your potential spouse. Some people still prefer the old-fashioned way to meet someone, and that's okay as well. Courting someone is an art form; you have to show them sides of you that you've never shown anyone before. You need to make sure they feel safe with you, miss you when you're not around, and cherish spending time with you. I can honestly say that my wife is the epitome of all of that. Living in the modern era, you don't have to have fancy weddings and all kinds of crazy shindigs to court someone. My wife and I eloped to Savannah, Georgia during St. Patrick's Day weekend. It was the most fun I've had with a single human being in my life. We ate at the Olde Pink House, laughed over drinks, and bonded like we never had before. What's amazing is that you realize all you need to make this work is each other. With some trust, faith, love, and patience, you can make your partnership last forever.

Marriage isn't easy, and neither is courting a partner to last for your whole life. Nothing in life that is easy will end up being what you're really looking for. I stand by that, because if it was so easy to marry the lady in your life, then you wouldn't have to work so hard to keep her. Appreciate a person who makes you work for some things, not everything in life is just given to you. Sometimes you have to put in work and earn that trust, love, and patience. People come from all different walks of life, and while it may be easy for you to accomplish certain goals, it may not be as easy for the person you're in a relationship with. Never judge a person by their current status in life – as long as they have goals and work to pursue them, give them a chance. I believe in giving love a chance. You never know who you may end up with or how it happens. Love is a funny thing, it can happen at the strangest time in our lives.

I personally believe in dating with a purpose, I have never been a fan of just dating for the hell of it. That's just me, that's how I roll. I think when you're with someone and you have no possibility of marrying them, then you're wasting your time. Dating should be your time to get to know who she is, what she likes, what she dislikes, what she wants to do, and how she sees her future with you. It should be a mutual feeling – if she doesn't see you as a part of her future, then you have to make the choice to wait around, convince her, or move on. These can be difficult choices to make when being faced with such a dilemma. It's important to decide if she is worth convincing or waiting around for. My wife felt like I was worth waiting for, and I'm glad she waited for me to propose to her. A lot of men wonder when the right time to propose is – trust me, you will know! You will realize that she is your better half, she completes you. And you can't really be the person you want to be without her.

Listen, my wife and I had briefly met my sophomore year of college when I was walking one of my friends back to her dorm after going out one night. My wife thought I was gay because I dressed nice and had walked a group of girls home with no desire to sleep with any of them. How crazy is that? If you are a gentleman and do the right thing, people will often just make assumptions about you without knowing what or who you are. My wife now admits that she was wrong for assuming that about me, but in her defense, a lot of college women's interactions with men are with people who only want to have sex with them. So when they come across a guy that doesn't try to pursue them sexually, they are taken aback by it. I think that's how a lot of women feel sometimes, that if you're a nice guy, then you're just being nice because you want sex, or else you're gay, because you have no interest in them. It is completely bizarre to just think that about someone solely based on the fact that they are being NICE! I have said this so many times, but I have to say it again. Kindness has become so rare in our society that people either think you're being a creep or you want something in return. It baffles me how we have let levels of civility and kindness get to this point. My wife wasn't the only girl in college to think this about me. Almost every encounter I had with a girl was the same, or else it was the exact opposite. I was often "friend-zoned" or taken advantage of because I was too nice, not cool at all. What ever happened to people appreciating a well-dressed, kind, and loving person? Can we just get back to that? I think we can.

It's funny how things work, because my senior year of college I re-met my wife (Meesh, which is short for Michele) through Alan's mutual friend Clay. I remember it like it was yesterday; Alan and I went to go meet up with Clay. She was eating with Clay and Kevin, and we sat down and talked for a while as we ordered food. Clay said, "Hey, Kelvin, this is Meesh. But she said she already met you once." I didn't recall meeting her at the time. I thought about how I would have known her, and it just didn't ring a bell until she mentioned her friends that I had walked home two years prior. She had been on the swim team at the time we first briefly met. The friend I'd walked home was also on the swim team, so they all knew each other and were friends, which made sense later as to how she knew I had never slept with her friend. As we ate, they were all drinking as well, but I decided not to, because I had bronchitis and was on antibiotics. Well, so was Meesh, as she said, "So, I'm drinking – and I'm also on antibiotics for bronchitis." I was thinking to myself, "Wow! She is drinking while taking medicine for bronchitis!" Little did I know that she would later be the mother of my kids and the love of my life.

We continued to hang out with the same mutual friends, Clay, Alan, Michael, and others. At the time we were both in relationships, so there was really no funny business between us. As time went on, I began to be interested in her and wanted to hang out more. My short-term relationship at the time ended because she didn't appreciate a nice dapper gentleman like myself. Meesh's also ended around the same time for similar reasons, he didn't really try to hang onto her or spend time with her. We fell for each other, and I asked her to go out on a date. I didn't have a car at the time, so she drove, but I paid for everything. We went to eat at Mucho Margaritas and saw Shutter Island. Over dinner, I remember her staring at me like I was insane for talking about my conspiracy theories about Atlantis and comparing the movie Avatar to the way Native Americans had lived prior to Mr. Columbus taking over their land. She thought I was interesting, and I wasn't afraid to be myself around her. I loved talking about what was on my mind, and she was a great listener.

We went out a few more times after that, and then decided to date more seriously. She was amazing, she got along with all my friends – we had mutual friends and went out with them a lot. Time flew by, and things got deep, really deep. We were going to be parents. Yeah, that's right – we had sex before marriage and she got pregnant! Now, before you close this book and start judging....listen. We did not intend to get pregnant, it just happened, and things happen for a reason. We were scared, happy, and nervous. I mean, we were both seniors in college and hadn't yet graduated. It took a while for her to break the news to her parents. But I had met her parents and some of her extended family before she became pregnant, so telling them wasn't as difficult as we thought, because they knew who I was and that we had a serious relationship. Nonetheless, that didn't make it any easier for her to break the news. She was nervous and timid and didn't know how they would react. Honestly, as a father now, I can't say how I would react in the same situation! I just wanted her family to know that I was going to stick by her and try my very best to be a provider and support her in any way possible. Eventually, after the dust settled and everyone came to the realization that the baby was coming, things got easier for us. As Alan, Devon, and Greg moved on to the new chapters in their lives, I was starting one also. Meesh and I decided to move in together and handle the situation we had been given.

We worked hard providing for our new family of three. Temperance was born January 20, 2011, and it was one of the greatest days of my life. It was even more amazing because Meesh graduated one month before she gave birth and walked across that stage nine months pregnant like the amazing lady she is – strong. I decided to take that semester off from school to work and save money to help out when the baby arrived. I started student teaching a few weeks before Temp was born; I was also working as a food runner and waiter at a local restaurant called Harper's. Simultaneously working as a waiter, student teaching, and becoming a first-time father was difficult, to say the least. We were poor, sleep-deprived, and in utter shock about the direction our lives had taken.

I wanted to marry her, and she wanted to be my wife, but I just wasn't ready and able to give her what she deserved. She deserved a house, consistent money, and less stress. But I was trying my best to make that happen! I worked so many hours that because of my already flat feet, my left foot began to give out on me to the point where I couldn't walk. If I couldn't walk, then I couldn't wait tables and make money for my family. It was a stressful time for me, because I had no income and Meesh was working three jobs just to help us survive. It was then that I knew she was the ONE! She held our family down while taking care of me after my foot surgery, which left me unable to walk for about three months. I was talking to my mother one day, and I told her that I wanted to propose to Meesh but I couldn't even walk. She deserved this huge proposal that I couldn't give her because I was broke; I literally had no money and could not walk at all.

When she came home, Meesh would always get me ice for my foot to help keep the swelling down after my surgery. Well, little did she know I had ordered an engagement ring and placed it in the freezer with a note that read, "Will you marry me?!" At this point after my surgery, I was able to at least hop on my good leg and use crutches to get around. Meesh came home from working her three jobs for the day, and I asked her to get me some ice for my foot. She replied, "But you're able to move around a little, you should try and get it." She clearly didn't suspect what I was up to. So, I just whined a little and said, "But you're already up, can you just grab some for me real fast?" Being the wonderful person she is, she went and fetched the ice for me. As soon as she opened the freezer, she just stood there, then she turned around and said with joy, "Are you serious?" I wasn't able to get down on one knee completely, so I put one knee down on the couch and waited for her. She had the note and ring in her hand – I looked her into her eyes and asked her to be my wife! It was one of the happiest moments of my life.

This woman who had been there for me through all the trials and tribulations chose to stick with me and make our situation work.

I am telling you the story of my proposal because there is no ideal way to do it. You just need to be genuine, heartfelt, and make it unique to you, the person she knows and loves. It's not about how big the ring is or how much the ring cost, it matters if you bought the ring with your heart, not with money. People get married every day, and people get divorced every day, and the size of the ring has nothing to do with either; it has everything to do with how you treat her, how you interact with her friends and family, and how you carry your love in the relationship. When you start dating, be a genuine gentleman; if you're driving when you go to pick her up, GET OUT OF THE CAR AND KNOCK ON THE DOOR!!! Do not wait in your car and honk your horn, or text her, "I'm outside." Going to her door shows the little bit of effort you're ready to make when dating her.

Everyone's financial situation is different, especially in the modern day, so it's okay to monetarily split things when going out and occasionally let her pay if she insists on it. If you don't have much money, then try to do things that don't cost. You can find plenty of things in your area to do for fun that don't involve breaking the bank. I personally never had to spend a lot of money on my wife when we dated. She enjoyed my company, so we would watch a lot of movies at our apartments, go swimming at our apartment pools, and hang out with our mutual friends. We had fun just being in each other's presence. That's the most important thing;

make sure you enjoy one another's presence, not presents! People love to give gifts and waste money on nonsense when in actuality that person probably just wants you to open up more, introduce them to your family, and show how much you care about them in ways other than with material items. Remember to simply be yourself! Don't pretend to be anything you're not – if she doesn't like you for you, then she's not the one. Don't change something you love about yourself to try to meet someone else's unrealistic standards.

I can tell you that the Art of Courtship and the Art of Being Your Own Man are one and the same. Own who you are, be proud of who you are, wear what makes you feel confident and comfortable. Make sure to be that guy you want your daughter to marry, and most importantly, be that guy that you want your son to be. Set good examples by opening up doors for people, helping others in need, and showing them random acts of kindness. Last but not least, be happy with her – if you aren't happy with her, then don't court her. Happiness is one of the main keys to life, make her happy and she will do the same in return. It's all about giving, not taking, being you, sacrificing, communicating, having patience, and loving them uncondishy. That's all you need to master the Art of Courtship, everything else will fall in place...trust yourself. Trust the journey and trust the process.

I've mastered a lot in my life, but love has mastered me. #OneLove

Stay ready, so you don't have to get ready!

Got hungry, so I had to scarf down some style

Chapter 8

Modeling Good Behavior

"Positivity is what made us famous."

– Lil' Yachty

A first impression is everything, especially when meeting a stranger. It's important to look presentable for the occasion while also being courteous. Kindness will get you a lot further in life than anything else will. People will remember you for how you looked, how you treated them, and most importantly, how you made them feel. It's vital to crush every first impression we have with another person. Now, if they have a preconceived thought about you based on what someone else has said, then there's nothing much you can do about that, other than to prove them wrong. Always remember that what people say about you is none of your business, and it says more about them than it ever will about you. Make sure they have something positive to say about you, whether it is the way you spoke, dressed, or approached them. Modeling good behavior in various circumstances in life will make you a more versatile gentleman, the kind of gentleman who can move with poise in a room full of vultures. I have done this a ton in my life; you never know when, where, or who you will meet, so it's best to be prepared for anything. This life can hand you anything, and it's your job to make the most of it. As the old saying goes, "When life hands you lemons, you squeeze those motherfuckers and make some lemonade."

Let's begin with style, because honestly, your clothing will attract people, but you want to make sure it attracts the right kind of people. After all, dressing well is a form of good manners. I believe every man should own a white dress shirt (of oxford cloth), brown shoes, and a well-tailored suit. The key word here is "well-tailored" – the way something fits says a lot about that person. If your suit does not fit well and looks sloppy and not well put together, then chances are people will assume that you don't really care. Listen, if people can see that you care about yourself, then they can see how you care for others. Self-love translates to love for others! If it's your first time buying a suit, I suggest going with a navy or grey color; these two colors are the most versatile for suiting. You can switch them depending on the occasion. As a bigger guy myself, I try to model good style behavior through being Notoriously Dapper. Mixing and matching various pieces like a grey blazer, white shirt, dark denim, and brown shoes is good for just about everything from a cocktail party or a date to a night out with your buddies. No matter the occasion, you always want to dress to impress. When I say impress, I mean impress others *and* yourself. Yes, yourself. Shock yourself and throw on something you've never worn before. You will be surprised how good you look in some types of clothing you've never before tried. Step outside your comfort zone and rock those red pants or that purple shirt.

Along with some style (which we will talk about a lot more later), you will need to be lingo versatile. I can personally hold a conversation with someone who is hood or with a person who is a CEO. That is the beauty of communication; when our judgments get in the way of how we treat others or talk to them, then we have lost our humanity. You have to know how to talk to people. Conversing well is a very important trait in life, from meeting a stranger to a job interview; you need to know what to say and when to say it. Of course we all have seen the comedy skits of black men who are talking in proper grammar, but then when their black counterparts greet them, their lingo changes a bit. As hilarious as these skits are, this is a very real dilemma that we often face on a daily basis. Being yourself will help you to conquer this and to be able to speak to anyone of any race, religion, or background. Truth be told, we are all human and we all speak different languages.

The most important language of all is our body language. How you dress, look, and speak all plays a role in that. Whether you are on a first date or a job interview or talking to a stranger, make sure you seem open. I know many of us are nervous or have social anxiety, and that can prevent you from being open. One thing you can do with your body language to help show your openness is to face the other person while conversing. If you face them, then it gives the impression that you are engaged in the conversation and want to listen to that person speak. Do you want to know how to tell when a conversation is about to end? When they start to reposition their body away from you, that's a clear sign that they are about to move on. Another way to ensure openness is by making eye contact; no, I'm not talking about some long deep romantic eye contact. I'm talking about simply looking at them while they are talking with you. The last thing you can do is say something simple during the conversation, like, "that's amazing", "wow", "that's really cool" or any positive response at all. Asking questions about the topic of discussion can also help show openness.

Now personally, I have a slight stutter when I talk. That's just the way I was made, and I embrace it. I was in speech classes for the majority of my life. So naturally I had some social anxiety growing up, because people teased me about my stuttering. As time went on and I got older, my speech improved. I still stutter and I'm almost 30. I have no shame about it. My brain knows what I'm going to say before I say it. Sometimes it's too fast for me to catch up, and I stumble over my words. Even though I have been faced with this adversity, I have still remained open and have a very social life. Self-love is about loving our perfect imperfections and embracing the challenges that come with them.

Modeling good behavior is also vital for your career. As a model, I can say that in any type of job you have, you must model good behavior. If you model good behavior, more people will want to be around you and have you in their circle, which may lead to those people keeping in contact with you for more time, new opportunities, or even promotions. When you work hard, show kindness, and help others, you can reach past your potential. I have been asked back to model for companies more than once because of my good behavior, willingness to work hard, and kindness. I have been told by many brands and companies that I'm such a pleasure and easy to work with. That's what you want! You want people to feel like it's a pleasure to hire you, hang out with you, or even converse with you.

I remember when I had my first modeling shoot ever; it was for Chubbies Shorts in Washington, D.C. On the plane, I met Cody, one of the other models; we exchanged a brief hello and acknowledged one another. We sat in separate seats on the plane ride, so we didn't get to talk much. After completing the plane trip from Atlanta to D.C., I was walking into the terminal only to be greeted by Cody. He waited for me to exit the plane so we could talk and ride together to the studio for the photo shoot. I was excited to not only meet a fellow model, but also to have someone to converse with on the way there to ease my nerves. I was very nervous! I had never modeled a day in my life, and I had no clue what to expect or anything. So I offered to pay for the taxi there, and he in turn offered to pay for the one back to the airport, which worked out perfectly.

When we arrived, I immediately saw cameras, props, and food. I walked in and was greeted by Mason, one of Chubbies' content creators; he's really nice and he welcomed me with open arms. We talked a little bit about my background and the trip over to D.C. This was my first time in D.C., and I loved the scenery. Cody and I were the last two models to show up, so it was show time. We were fitted and dressed, then shot some amazing content. We even did a Victoria's Secret angel spoof! We were shirtless, wearing angel wings in the middle of D.C. during the winter. My nipples were freezing, but it was worth every bit of cold breeze. I met some amazing guys, and we became "Mangels"; we took pictures with a bunch of random people who were looking on with curious eyes everywhere, wondering, "What the heck are these guys doing with angel wings on and no shirts?" Mason told me what a good sport I was and how much he enjoyed having me be a part of that photo shoot.

Everything went well because of my positive attitude and good behavior, so well that I have modeled for Chubbies numerous times now. I have been to San Francisco, Palm Springs, and Lake Tahoe because they enjoy my company on a shoot that much. I look forward to more travels and photo shoots with them. Being fortunate enough to travel places I have never been makes it that much more fun. The bad side of modeling, though, is the lack of diversity in the fashion industry.

Modeling good behavior is also about how you handle defeat and negativity. Like anything else, it's never going to be all sunshine and rainbows. You will encounter people you don't like or agree with who have negative attitudes. How you handle them will test your good behavior. Not too long ago, I was at a wedding where I encountered some older guests who were very conservative and clearly "pro-Trump". I personally disagreed with them on their political views, but it did not stop me from having a casual conversation with them. My wife mentioned to me later that evening how much she admired my ability to keep my composure when talking to Trump supporters. Truth be told, I don't care what your political views are as long as you have a good heart and do right by people. Occasionally you are going to encounter that person who is fueled by hate and negativity. The easiest way to handle them is to simply smile and kill them with kindness. Sometimes you may have to walk away to avoid escalation of the situation. The last thing anyone wants is to get into a physical altercation with someone over words. The older we get, the more we realize that there are alternative ways to handle certain confrontations. Be mature; use your discretion when reacting to the negativity of others. Remember, we can't control anyone else but ourselves – take control and use that good behavior to show others positivity.

We often forget that others are influenced by the way we act. I see it too often in the middle school where I teach, young kids idolize these musical artists who vocalize about murder, sex, and talking to women like they're objects. It is one thing to be an entertainer, but it's another thing to be a role model, especially a good role model. Not everyone is cut out to do it, and that's unfortunate. We have a lot of famous people that our young kids look up to for guidance and reassurance. Sometimes instead of guidance and reassurance, what they get is trapping, gang banging, and violence. On the flip side, we have excellent role models in pro athletes, music artists, and television personalities. I just personally wish the younger kids *liked* more positive role models.

During New York Fashion Week: Men's I had the chance to meet Lil' Yachty. I kind of had an inkling he was going to be in attendance since I'd heard he would be taking over as Nautica's creative director for a year. I went into the Nautica presentation, and as I was walking around, I heard a commotion starting up. I looked over, and it was the BOAT himself – Lil' Yachty! He was dressed in head to toe Nautica gear, repping the new Fall/Winter line. As he was taking pictures and giving interviews, there was a certain glow about him. I could tell he wasn't like the rest of the rappers I had met. He is young, but genuine; his aura was pure. After the CEO of Nautica showed him around the presentation and gave him a run-through of the new collection, he was free to chat and take pictures with his fans. Being a hip-hop fan myself as well as a middle school teacher, it's safe to say I knew who he was. I also knew how much of a positive influence he had on my students. So, I decided to go up and talk to him.

I walked up to him, gave him a dap hug, and proceeded to chitchat with him. Our conversation was engaging and very enlightening. Before our conversation ended, I asked him if he would do me a favor. He said, "Sure, man. What's up?" I explained to him who I was and what I did for a living. He was impressed that I was holding down so many jobs (coach, teacher, model, blogger, author, husband and father). I then told him how much my students at St. Andrews loved him and asked him if he would be willing to say hey to them and show them some love. He was all about it, and I knew then that he was something special, something that the new generation needed in a world full of negative influences. As I took out my phone and went to video mode, he gently took the phone away from me and said, "Hey, hey, hey, what's up to everybody at St. Andrews Middle School in Columbia, South Carolina. I got a lot of family in North Carolina, so I got mad love for y'all in South Carolina. You guys got an amazing teacher here, man. Rocking out and looking real fly. So, big shout-out to everybody, man! And I love y'all."

It made my day to have that video ready to show my students when I returned from Fashion Week. They went ABSOLUTELY NUTS when they saw the video. It was a moment of instant gratification for them. Someone they idolized, looked up to, and wanted to be like had acknowledged them and their presence. It brought pure joy to my heart to see the smiles and positive reactions on their faces. It's safe to say that Lil' Yachty is definitely a modern day young gentleman. He was nice and courteous and he showed genuine love to his fans. Being an entertainer can be stressful and very tiresome, but I admire that young man for handling his fame while using his platform to promote positivity. He has a long, bright future ahead; I wish him nothing but the best in life and in the industry!

As an educator, coach, model, and now author, I have a responsibility to continue being a positive role model for this generation. I have always used the word "strong" to refer to anything positive. I use it so much that many of my friends, family, and coworkers have also started using the term. It can be used in any way, as long as it represents something positive. For example, when someone says, "Hey, how are you?" You can reply to them by saying "I'm good, strong." The key is to use it at the end of a statement to put emphasis on the positivity associated with the words. Like, "I went to go get some tacos after work, strong." Or "I'm going out on a date tonight, strong." I also use it as a substitute for any positive affirmation. When someone says something positive like, "I got this shirt on sale," I say, "Strong!" to put a positive affirmation on what they said. The word has gotten around so strong now that I have my entire school, teachers, students and administrators saying "STRONG". It has added so much positivity to the school's environment. Even when I waited tables, my coworkers also used it as term of positive influence. Be that strong positive influence and role model for your friends, family, and coworkers. Believe it or not, the things we do and say influence people. So it's important as a modern day gentleman to model good behavior, not just for your future, but also for the future of our generation. Model behavior that is unforgettable (in a good way), not unforgivable! Keep finding the positive in negative situations, and continue being the guy everyone wants to hire, promote, and be around.

An Ivory suit on Ebony skin is always a win!

Always let the light inside you shine brighter than the light shining on you!

I know sometimes life gets hard, but smile today for a better tomorrow.

20 Things Every Man Should Know About Weddings & Style

There is going to be a time for each of us when we will be invited to a wedding. Whether you're invited as a wedding guest or a plus-one, there is some simple etiquette you should know. I'm going to give you a list of eight things to help you be the best wedding guest or wedding date around.

Dress appropriately, I can't stress this enough. There is nothing worse than a guy showing up to an event not dressed correctly. Do whatever you have to do beforehand to make sure you look up to par for the wedding. Pay attention to the dress code; if the invite says black tie optional, then that what it means. It's an option for you to dress black tie, but honestly, when in doubt, wear a damn navy suit, white oxford shirt, and brown shoes. As long as you don't show up in shorts and a tank top (unless otherwise stated by the wedding party), then you should be good to go.

Come to the wedding prepared. The second worst thing after dressing inappropriately is showing up half dressed. Being the Notoriously Dapper gentleman I am, I know how to tie a bow tie and necktie. It is shocking to me how many guys don't know how to do either. I have had to tie ties for people at weddings. Honestly, in my opinion it looks bad when you show up to a wedding with an untied tie in your hand searching for someone to tie your tie. It's not a good look. Try and be more prepared when you're attending a wedding. Don't show up with an untied tie, unlaced shoes, untucked shirt, etc. Take a few seconds to just get your attire together.

Remember people will remember two things about you: how you looked (whether appropriate or inappropriate) and how you made them feel, good or bad.

Once you've got the look down, then you need to show up ON TIME! Don't be that wedding guest who rolls in after the bride has walked down the isle. Do your very best to be on time. It's a plus for you, because you get to find a good seat and chat a little bit with some people you will be spending the evening with at the reception. On top of showing up on time, make sure you don't show up empty-handed. At least give them a card congratulating them on their wedding. This may vary though, sometimes the wedding party will insist that no one bring gifts; in that case, don't worry about it. I personally think it's a nice gesture to at least give them a card with a few kind words. People cherish things of that sort.

Mingle your way around and meet some of the wedding guests. This is a great way to meet new people from various parts of the world. You have nothing to be shy about, because you all are there for the same reason, to watch two people wed. Whether you know the bride or the groom, it's nice to meet their friends and other family members. When mingling, keep the conversation light with strangers; stay away from offensive topics like politics, religion, and so forth. Now, if you're with your own friends at the wedding, then you all can have your own conversation about whatever, but keep in mind that there are many other people in attendance. You don't want the sister, cousin, uncle, or dad to hear something that they can be offended by. Keep it simple and mingle gracefully.

Always find a way to meet the parents of the bride and groom to congratulate them on the wedding. It's good manners for you as a guest to introduce yourself to both parties' parents. Keep it simple and don't give them unwanted information, just tell them how much you appreciate being in attendance and how beautifully everything turned out. If they choose to ask you more questions, then proceed to talk with them about whatever it may be – football, weather, places and travel, etc. Make sure you're attentive during the conversation, and don't forget their names. Parents usually spend a lot of money on these occasions, so be sure to make it a priority to meet them before the wedding or reception is over.

Attend to your plus-one if you have one – the wedding invitation will let you know if you may invite a plus-one. Don't bring a plus-one if you don't have permission to bring one! Being a plus-one to a wedding guest can be awkward if you don't really know the wedding party. Some people bring friends, new girlfriends, and more. Whoever you bring as your plus-one, be sure to attend to them. Introduce them to some of the wedding guests that you know already. Don't leave them solo in a conversation with someone they don't know. If they are running low on beer or wine, offer to refill it for them. Make them feel like they are your plus-one. You can accomplish this in various ways, talking to them with other wedding guests, eating with them, dancing together, and more. If you don't have the intention of treating your plus-one *as* a plus-one, then you don't need to bring them. It would be a waste of their time and yours as well. Pick your plus-one wisely.

Don't drink too much or get drunk. If the wedding has an open bar or any alcohol, be sure to drink responsibly. Don't be that person who gets shitfaced like they're still a freshman in college and ruins the reception. If you feel as if you're getting too drunk, then stop drinking and have some water for a bit. I have heard personal stories of drunken friends and family ruining occasions like weddings and receptions. It's not cool in any way. You don't have to stay completely sober, just don't get black-out drunk; find a happy medium and keep it classy.

Last but definitely not least, DANCE and HAVE FUN! No matter what the DJ or band is playing, just get up and dance. Dancing is good for the heart and soul. If you have a plus-one, make sure you dance with them! Treat them special. You should also be dancing in celebration of the wedding party. After all, a wedding is a celebration of two people who love each other and intend to spend the rest of their life together. That right there is beautiful and should be reason enough for you to dance. If you're worrying about the fact that you "can't dance" – dance anyway. Trust me, NO ONE is concerned if you can or can't dance. Everyone will be in their own world enjoying themselves. Join the party on the dance floor and just dance, dance, dance, dance...can't stop the feelinggggggg, so just dance, dance, dance, dance.

Now that we got those things squared away, let's move on to some style tips. I believe fashion is nothing but a bunch of silly trends that fade in and out. Style is forever; style is tangible, and tells the world who you are. I am going to give twelve things I think every man should have in his wardrobe. These items can be worn interchangeably and matched any way you want to style them. Without any more delay, let's get into it.

The Oxford Shirt: Every man should have at least one white oxford shirt. I prefer the traditional American oxford shirts with the buttons on the collar. When you find a brand and fit you like, I suggest stocking up on colors like black, grey, blue, and one statement color (pink, purple, red) or pattern. These shirts are so versatile, they can be dressed up or down and worn with anything from suits to casual outfits. They fit just about any and every occasion imaginable, and they will never let you down when you are in need of something to wear. They are a mandatory staple to have in your wardrobe. I suggest getting at least two white oxford shirts so you can change them out periodically and not have to rely on just one!

A Navy Suit: Whether you need it for an interview, job, or wedding, this is the best investment to make when buying a suit. Navy is forever; it will NEVER go out of style. Make sure it's well tailored and fitted. Many men buy suits and don't realize they need some minor alterations done. Listen, details matter. The arm length of the suit, the size of the jacket, and the length of the pants defines good and bad suits. When you find the right fit for your body (go to a tailor and find that right fit), you will then find out how versatile a navy suit is. It looks good on everyone, every skin tone, size, and age. You can dress it all the way up with an oxford shirt, tie, and brown shoes. Or you can dress it down with a tee shirt and sneakers. You can even wear the pants and jacket as separates. The possibilities are endless with a good navy suit. This should always be your first color of suit to purchase. The second should be grey, but for now play it safe and do navy. You cannot and will not go wrong. Trust me...look at my book cover!

Dark Denim Jeans: In case you haven't noticed, I'm all about versatility and what the clothes can do for you. Dark denim, just like an oxford shirt and navy suit, can be worn with just about anything. I'm telling you, an oxford shirt and dark denim are an endless combination. A good pair of denim jeans can be hard to come across, so when you find the right size and fit...buy them. They will last you forever! I've been wearing the same pair of dark denim for almost 3 years now. Just like the other items I have listed so far, dark denim jeans can be dressed up or down for just about any occasion.

The Everyday Bag: We all need an everyday bag to carry our personal belongings in. Most guys carry a messenger bag or tote. Whatever suits your style, just make sure you look for two things: its durability and whether or not it's functional. I'm a firm believer in quality over quantity. I would rather have one great everyday bag that lasts me forever and is reliable than have five that do not. Always go with quality, it's never about how many you have but how long it lasts.

I suggest going with good leather (rugged or chic) for the material. Make sure you take a look at the inside and see if you can fit what you need into it as well. Nothing worse than having a bag that can't hold your laptop, papers, or whatever else you need to carry that day. Don't get a bag just because it looks good. Get a bag that looks good *and* will be functional and last for a while.

A Nice Timepiece: Nothing says how mature you are more than the watch you wear. Invest in a good timepiece, and actually use it for telling the time. There is nothing more confusing than someone looking at their phone for the time when they are wearing a watch. Your timepiece should provide both function and style. I would advise getting a timepiece that will go with just about anything, a white face with a leather band is the most versatile. A leather band can be dressy or casual depending on what you wear with it. Naturally, if you wear a suit it will be dressy, if you wear something casual like a T-shirt and jeans, then it would be more casual. Either way, a nice timepiece will turn heads, complement your outfit, and make you look mature.

Chelsea Boots: I am a sucker for some Chelsea boots. They are easy to slip on and off, come in an array of styles, and look good with EVERYTHING! Personally, I have a black pair, a brown pair, and a pink suede pair. What I love most about the Chelsea boot is it's a year round shoe. Don't get me wrong, I love lace-up boots too, but when you're on a time schedule and you just want to get well dressed and leave, the Chelsea boot is the answer. Make sure you find a style that fits your personal preference. If you like a rounded toe, then go with that, and so forth. The styles are endless; just make sure you get a quality pair that doesn't hurt your feet.

Khakis/Chinos: These items are lifesavers. When you don't feel like wearing denim or suit pants, you wear chinos. They come in many colors and styles as well. I personally like mine with some stretch in them – my thighs are big, so I love having the extra flexibility when I'm moving. I have six pair of chinos, two black pairs, two khaki, one olive, and one navy. Sometimes I wear them with an oxford and blazer or with a T-shirt. Chinos are awesome because they offer a good alternative to denim. They work just like denim but don't give such a casual vibe. Of course you can wear them with sneakers or dress shoes and make it work with a casual or more dressy look.

Brown Dress Shoes: I say brown, because to me black is very very limited. Brown is much more universal and versatile. Now, there are many styles of dress shoes, from cap toe, wingtip, and brogues to monk straps. Honestly, pick a style that works for you and own it. I recommend going with a medium shade of brown (not too dark, not too light). That way, if you wear a lighter shade of brown belt or a darker shade of brown belt, it won't contrast as much. When you have a white oxford shirt, a well-fitted navy suit, and some brown shoes...you can feel damn near invincible. The nice timepiece will elevate your look that much more!

Polo Shirt: They are like T-shirts with collars, just think of them as a more elegant version of a T-shirt. What's good about polo shirts is that almost every brand makes them.

There are nearly endless options, and I advise free range when picking a polo. You really need to find that right fit though. Guess what? You can wear a polo with a suit as well. It's very versatile for various weather situations as well. If you want to pop the collar, go ahead and do that too. I did in high school, and I owned it. Every man needs a polo shirt in their wardrobe. I would suggest getting one solid color and one pattern. That way you have options if you want to try something...spicier.

A Leather Jacket: This is an absolute must, everyone looks cool as shit in a leather jacket. The best place to find them is in a thrift store or consignment shop. I tell you, I have seen some amazing ones in thrift stores. I remember the feeling I got when I received my first leather jacket. I felt like a super hero (kind of how I felt when I saw the Black Panther trailer) – straight up savage. I recommend getting a black leather jacket, although I have seen some really cool brown and colored ones. I feel as though black is so strong, timeless and badass. That's just my opinion though! Wear what makes you feel great.

Sport Coat/Denim Jacket: I put both down because you can really use either one. If you invest in a navy suit, then you can use the navy blazer as a sport coat and invest in a denim jacket, whatever wash you prefer, I would stay away from the really ripped up ones with holes everywhere, solely because you will be wearing it in public, and the chances of it getting caught in something and ripping more is very high. Having the option of a denim jacket will help your style game; when you don't want to wear a blazer or leather jacket...wear a denim jacket. It will serve the same purpose and get the job done.

All White Sneakers: This is last because honestly, it's VERY important to me. I didn't realize how important all white shoes were until last year, when I was getting dressed and couldn't find the right shoes to wear. I put on my all white Stan Smith's, and the whole outfit came together. You can wear these shoes with just about anything, from a suit, to a T-shirt, to a denim jacket. The possibilities are infinite with white sneakers. Make sure you wipe them down every once in a while when they get dirty. Keep them classy and clean.

These 12 items should help you start a base and elevate your wardrobe. Any guy can pull these items off. You just need to have confidence and find the right fit. Also, don't be afraid to go to a tailor and get things altered. It's okay to be picky and get those extra inches taken up or let out. Be sure to look through your closet, because you probably already have most of these items and just didn't know how to pair them correctly. Always remember, the most important outfit is self-confidence...wear it and own it. #StyleHasNoSize

They say a well-tailored suit is to women what lingerie is to men. #Truth

I've got 99 problems but suits ain't one

I put the O and the G in GROOMING ha-ha!

If I were a fruit, I'd be a fineapple

Making my way downtown, walking fast. Faces pass and I'm homebound!
#WhereIsTerryCrewsWhenYouNeedHim

Chapter 9

Behavior at the Workplace

"Either I can teach you how to behave, or life can. It's your choice."

– Dad

In the modern day, there are a variety of work environments, from the cool chill spots of tech companies to strict law firm culture. Wherever you work, whether it's laid-back or strict, you need to know how to behave. Personally, I've bumped heads with people at work before. I feel as though that's a pretty common thing. Think about it this way: in the workplace, you have people from all walks of life and backgrounds. To say you are going to get along with everyone you work with just isn't feasible. You will not like certain things about some people, but others will compensate for those negatives by being your work friends. You know, that friend you meet at work who is cool as shit, and you pretty much like doing everything with them, including work. The workplace can be a stressful environment, depending on your employer and what you do for a living. To make work easier for you, understand that you will have to obey the job rules, go out of your way to help coworkers, and just simply be nice.

Being nice will get you VERY far in life, trust me. The biggest problem with younger professionals in the workplace is that they don't want to follow the rules and stay in their lane. They have been told all their life that everyone else is wrong and to break those rules. Don't get me wrong, I'm all about breaking the rules and changing things in ways that you believe in, but there is a time and place for that. The workplace is not the place to start preaching about your beliefs, because honestly, let's face it; someone is going to disagree with you. You are going to lose some respect or possibly create a conflict if the topic is sensitive (gay rights, religion, women's rights). It's best to keep most personal feelings to yourself while at work. The last thing any of us want is someone, especially our bosses, questioning our competence because of something we said during a casual conversation at work. Let your work ethic do the talking. Don't talk about what you used to do or what you want to do. Just do you while working the hardest you can.

I have worked at all kinds of jobs, from retail and grocery stores to restaurants. Currently, I work as a middle school art teacher. Yeah, that's right – MIDDLE SCHOOL! I know what you all are thinking: "God bless you, man," "Damn, how do you put up with them?" or my favorite one of all, "People should get paid extra just to teach middle school." Unfortunately, you don't make a lot of money being an educator in America. I went to school for years, racked up student loans, and now work to pay them off by educating our youth.

I love being a teacher. It's one of the greatest things besides fatherhood to me. I would be lying if I told you I wanted to teach forever. I don't want to do it forever, but for now I enjoy it. I love art – always have and always will. As a kid, I would draw Beavis and Butthead in the bible during church (obviously I was bored). I can't even begin to explain how much my sister and I had to sneak around just to get a peek at that show. We would go to extremes to watch it; we were clearly successful, because I was so fascinated by the show that I drew the characters during church in a bible (old lady eye roll). I would often get into trouble during school for drawing various cartoon characters instead of paying attention and completing work sheets during class. I loved drawing and still do, so I turned my passion into a job.

When I was in high school, I excelled in art and took a variety of classes such as graphic design, photography, and even ceramics. I hated working with clay, but I respect any artist who can make magic with it! It takes a special person to make art out of clay, and I am not that special individual. It also takes a special individual to teach – and not many can do that either. Teaching requires patience, tons of improvising, self-reflection, and constant growth of knowledge. Each day is a different day. Students change attitudes and work ethics more often than my daughter changes shoes (which is a ton). One day you may have an attentive class with everyone on task and participating – then the next day you may have the class from hell. I feel as though most jobs work this way, right? No matter where we work, there are good days and bad days. When you're having one of those bad days, it's good to have a work friend or someone you trust to vent to. Holding your feelings in, no matter how small, is not mentally healthy for anyone.

Like I mentioned before, having a work friend is necessary for most people to survive hectic or long work days and weeks. I'm naturally an extrovert and have been since I was a kid. I don't really get shy around strangers, I try to find a way to talk to anyone. Having that kind of personality helps me at work. Due to my uplifting extroverted personality, many of my colleagues are excited to see me when I'm there. I often speak to them upon arrival, greeting everyone I see with a "good morning" followed by something positive like "strong" or "have a good day". Believe it or not, something that simple can change someone's mood for the better. I try to keep that kind of positive energy around at work, because you never know when you may need it on the receiving end. You have to give in order to receive; many forget that in this day and age. Always give positivity. Karma works, trust me. Do something nice for your coworkers from time to time. On a Monday after a long break, bring in some donut holes and a container of coffee just to get people through the day. The more you spread the positive and pay it forward, the more things will work out for you in the long run.

I have been working since I turned 15 years old. My first job was assisting a landscaper who went to my cousin's church. That job was grueling, but it paid well! For a kid, I was making some pretty big bucks (all cash too). Having that job taught me a lot about work ethics and being a humble employee. That job also set the tone for my attitude towards other jobs in my life. In college, I worked as a butcher in an organic grocery store. That job reminded me a lot of my first job. I had to do a lot of physical labor and dealt with a lot of shitty customers. Truth be told, I needed to work those jobs in order to appreciate what I have now. Although being a middle school teacher is mentally grueling, at least I'm not still in the same place I was at 15.

Life is all about progress, we should always get better at what we do. Speaking of progression, don't you hate those colleagues who have worked countless years in a career field and constantly brag about it? Look, it is one thing to be proud of your accomplishments in your line of work, but it's another thing to brag about it. Honestly, as an educator, I hate it when people rub in the fact they have taught for X number of years and this is how it should be done. Just because you've worked longer doesn't necessarily mean you know better. Times change, people change, technology has changed everything in the work world. Staying current with the times and adapting to change is what makes you excel in your career. Things are not always going to be smooth nor go your way. You will have to improvise and find a new way to do some things...that aspect of the world is just inevitable. It's going to happen, so be prepared for it. Change is good.

Sometimes when change occurs, people can't handle it. They freak out and let their emotions get the best of them. Don't be emotional about work, and definitely don't let work you emotional. Remember, it's just a job. Life is more than just working and paying rent, we all have a gift to embrace. It's easier said than done...trust me, I know. I can't tell you how many times I have come home an emotional wreck from work, but maybe my wife can, considering she's the one who has had to listen to me complain about it time and time again. She often reminds me that everything will be okay and it will all work out. She's right, it usually does find a way to work itself out. Sometimes we need that reminder to not let work get the best of us.

Embrace change, especially at work, because chances are you will experience it. Keep your composure and remain professional at all times, even though it can be hard to do in some circumstances. As an educator, you deal with all kinds of children from different walks of life. Some have guidance at home and some don't, it is what it is. I have personally had students curse me out and try to fight me, and even worse, parents trying to do the same. So you mean to tell me I'm getting cursed out by you due to writing your child a discipline referral for sticking their middle finger up at me and saying "fuck you" to me in a classroom? Sometimes you want to step back and let people know how "left" you can go. 'Don't let the bow ties fool you' type of stuff, you know. But we have to always remain professional! As one of my other favorite Michelles says, "When they go low, we go high." Always keep that mentality when dealing with foolishness in the workplace and circumstances in life; there are all kinds of crazy people in this world, unfortunately misery loves misery.

My parents have always encouraged me to follow my dreams. Dreams usually reflect passions, and passions can turn into work. I can say there was a time that I wanted to be a teacher, so I worked towards that goal and accomplished it. But as we grow, so do our dreams – it has always been my dream to be a well-known fashion icon! Sometimes you have to make a decision, it's either one day or day one. In February 2013, I decided to choose day one. Day one of Notoriously Dapper has turned into year four of Notoriously Dapper. Imagine if I was still telling others and myself, "Well, one day I'm going to start a blog." You control your dreams and how you go after them, no one else can throw you off track if you want it enough. The thing is, you have to want it as bad as you want to breathe. When you want it that badly, it will happen for you. Work your passion! If you work your passion, then you won't feel like you're working a day in your life. Doing what you love is mandatory, even if you have to work another job until you make it to your dream job. Do it, opportunities come to those who make them. Set yourself up to realize those dream-like passions we all have. When I started blogging, I did a lot of work for free to create opportunities while building relationships with brands and PR companies. Creating those relationships opened the doors for me to become a model, a high-profile influencer, and now an author! You should take every job as a chance to learn and use your experiences as information to prosper from later in life.

When you get a chance, simply sit down and set some goals for yourself. After you write them down, relax and reflect on what you can do to turn those goals into a job. Find that sweet spot when you can land your dream job, because honestly, if you work hard enough, eventually it will come. I never thought that I would turn my blog into a brand or be featured in *Glamour Magazine* and BuzzFeed. All of that seemed so far away from what I was doing when I began teaching. Now that I'm working both of my passions, it can be difficult to balance everything. I know eventually I will be able to blog and influence full time, I just have to keep working at it. As I rap, "Can't stop, won't stop Roc-A-Fella records, 'cause we get down, we get downnnnn. The girls, the girls they love us. 'Cause we stay fresh to death, we the best, nothing less". Teaching will always be an option for me down the road. I love educating our youth while providing them a positive influence. That's what this book is doing, right? Educating our young men to be better, succeed, have confidence, and dress well.

If you have a good character, then you shouldn't have to worry too much about behavior in the workplace. Be nice, speak to someone upon arrival, remain professional, dress well – and did I mention just be fucking NICE! If you can do that while staying in your own lane and focusing on your job, you will excel in the workplace without any question whatsoever. Control your emotions, don't speak on personal issues, and dress appropriately while working. Remember, professionalism is a major key, and what better way to say 'I'm professional' than dressing the part. Be punctual; if you're going to be late to work, then let someone know at your job. Communication helps prevent misunderstandings. Pay it forward, you never know when you may need to be on the receiving end of some good advice, a good deed, or a simple gesture to ensure we make it through the day. No matter where we work, what we do for a living, or what our passion is in life, we must remember to treat everyone with respect and kindness. Just because you're a supervisor or someone's boss doesn't give you the right to treat anyone, especially your employees, in an unkind way. That is not okay and should never be your behavior in the workplace. Continue to be kind and work hard, everyone can appreciate someone who does that. If they don't, well then, they don't appreciate good people when they see them. Honestly, that's not your problem, it's theirs. Just do you, that's the most authentic thing we can do in this life, STRONG!

Recap: 7 Basics About Behavior in the Workplace

1. Show up to work on time. Being punctual is an asset in the workplace. It helps keep a productive time management schedule for you and your coworkers.

2. Dress professionally. Do not violate the work dress code, and if you have a uniform, wear it. Always remember the impression you make at work is everything in this life. Make it a good one.

3. Mind your own business, worry about yourself, and do your job. Don't worry about others and what they do in the workplace. Be the best employee you can be.

4. Always have respect for others despite their age or how long they have been working there. Respect all your coworkers, say hello and good morning, and make sure you converse with them daily.

5. Be a team player. Remember to work together with your coworkers. When you work against each other, you don't accomplish much. Collaborate and learn from one another.

6. Follow the rules and regulations at your job. They are there for a reason; just follow them while you're at

work. When you get off, you don't have to worry about it anymore. It's only temporary.

7. Just be FUCKING NICE! Yes, I said it again. Be nice to the people you work with, work around, or that you have to deal with. Keep your composure in hot moments. Being nice and having charm and kindness is the key to a happy life, especially at the workplace!

I'm wearing reading rainbow

I often have to step out of my comfort zone to help spread the message of self-love! #ConfidenceIsKey

Don't put the con in conversing! #BePositive

Chapter 10

Marriage, Money & Morality

"Better late than never but never late is better. They say time is money, well, we'll spend it together."

- Drake

Life is filled with decisions we all must face in some way or another. Who are you going to marry? What job are you going to take? Where are you going to college? What are you going to major in? Need I go on? What makes us unique is our ability to use our own judgment to make these decisions. We may write down pros and cons to weigh our options, wishing to make the best possible choice for ourselves. What we do in our relationships, what we do with our money, and what we do with our lives is all about morality. Morality is the distinction between what's right or wrong. Not all your choices will be right and not all of your choices will be wrong. Sometimes you may get caught up in a catch-22, which can force you to make a brash decision in the event of internal conflict. It's like deciding whether to go to Carolina or Clemson – they are both awesome schools, but whichever one you choose, your allegiance during the Palmetto Bowl had better be strong. Orange has always been my least favorite color anyway, so it was a no-brainer for me to choose Carolina.

For real, though – people are faced with catch-22's all day, every day, and there sometimes can be crappy circumstances. That's life; we have to deal with what comes our way in the best way possible, whether that means you hurt people unintentionally along the way or not. You must always do what's best for you and your family...always. Never settle for anything less. When you decide to get married and wed that beautiful person you want to spend the rest of your life with, you need to remember just that. It is for the rest of your life; when they say "till death do us part," that's exactly what it means. Some people don't understand what those words mean, that you need to work through difficult times and grow together as one. Marriage IS NOT easy at all. It's not supposed to be, there will be rough patches. You're supposed to work with each other, becoming better people as you grow and potentially start a new life together. My wife and I have had our moments, but we continue to grow each day in our marriage.

When just the two of us decided to elope to Savannah, Georgia, close to St. Patty's Day weekend, we knew we wanted to spend the rest of forever together. I remember it like it was yesterday; I was wearing my green Cole Haan Air Colton wingtips and a custom-made navy suit. My wife wanted me to get dressed first, then go downstairs to wait in the hotel lobby. When I was headed downstairs, I texted her, "I'm coming down!" As I was heading down, she was going up to get dressed for our private ceremony. We had both agreed to not see each other before our elopement and to meet downstairs both dressed to surprise one another.

I was waiting downstairs for about an hour and a half, pacing back and forth, going inside and out again, then sitting down staring at my green wingtips hoping she was going to like them (her favorite color is green). I had prepared my vows weeks beforehand, so I was standing around reading them while pacing and pacing through the hotel lobby, mumbling the words as I was walking, probably looking like a complete nut-bag at that point. A well-dressed nut-bag, but nonetheless a nut-bag. My phone vibrated, and for the first time in foreverrrrrrr ('Frozen' style), I was nervous to look at it. What if it was just a random text? What if it was her saying she's coming down? I pulled out my phone with so much anticipation. I looked down at it, and it was my Dad, sending me his good wishes. I guess as a married man he could relate to having nervous guts before jumping the broom. I needed that text, it helped take the edge off my nerves. I knew everything was going to be fine after he texted me, it reassured me that what I was feeling was normal.

Then I got the "I'm coming down!" text, and finally the moment had arrived. I waited in front of the elevators, heart racing like a cheetah chasing its prey, while with each elevator door that opened, I got more and more nervous. After about three or four elevator doors opening, my anticipation grew more keen. Finally elevator number two opened up, and there she was – my Michele, looking beautiful, stunning, and simply breathtaking in her wedding dress. I was straight-up in awe, it was like I was seeing her for the first time all over again. Overwhelmed with butterflies, I walked up to her and told her how beautiful she was. We hugged, and it was like nothing I had ever felt before; pure love. We had made it so far in our relationship. She was the mother of my daughter, my lover, my partner, my better half....and simply my everything. We were about to face forever hand in hand in the name of love, and it felt so right. We walked out of the hotel, getting "hoorays," "congratulations," and high-fives everywhere we walked.

As we were walking to Forsyth Park to meet up with Rev. Schulte and our photographer, we realized if we kept walking at the same pace, then we wouldn't be able to meet them in time! So we quickly flagged down a taxi and told him to take us to Forsyth Park quickly, which he did gladly. We arrived in time for the ceremony with Rev. Schulte. Upon arrival, Michele and I were looking for him around the park. After looking for a few minutes, we found him chatting with his photographer near the fountain, which they had just finished dying green for the St. Patrick's Day festivities. It was beautiful, with green water shooting out everywhere; people from all over the park were crowding into that area to take pictures and whatnot. So we decided to move to a more secluded part of the park where we could share our vows and finally tie the knot.

As we were walking and talking with Rev. Schulte and his photographer, he mentioned to me how well we looked. I must admit we looked very good and felt even better. After walking for a bit and scouting some good locations, we picked a spot somewhat near the fountain so as to get pictures of it in the background. Rev. Schulte asked us if we were ready, we said yes, and he started the process. He started with me first; I began to read the vows that I had prepared (which were pretty much a book). I spent a good bit of time reading them, getting lost in my words as I was trying not to stutter. Michele had tears of joy rolling down her face. I closed my vows by telling her how much she meant to me as the mother of my child and better half. Michele wiped the tears from her face and started speaking her vows. They were touching and made me feel like a man she not only wanted but needed. It ended with Rev. Schulte finishing it off by officially declaring us husband and wife! We hugged, then I kissed my bride with pride. While we were taking our post-elopement pictures, our party was crashed by a group of very smelly hippies with cats crawling all over them. One had a ukulele and started singing us a song about being awesome. It is one of the best photos we have of that day.

You don't need to have a fancy wedding and spend all kinds of unnecessary money to marry the person you love. At the time, my wife and I didn't have much money at all, but we made do with what we had. We knew we couldn't afford a wedding, nor did we want to try. My wife is a bit of a homebody introvert and doesn't like having attention on her. So the whole bridezilla type thing just wasn't who she was, and I was happy about that. But anyhow, back to money. When you get married, money becomes a part of what you will share as a couple. Unfortunately, that's just the way life is. Everything costs money, food, gas, clothes, housing, and so on.

My wife and I experienced the struggle of being two new parents working dead-end jobs after college. I worked full-time as a waiter and food runner at Harper's Restaurant, while my wife worked three jobs every week; she taught Spanish lessons and swim lessons and also worked at a dry cleaner. We did what we had to do to survive. We didn't have much, but we had each other. We worked our asses off just to live in a 500 square foot cottage and barely ate good meals. Thankfully, I sometimes got free food at the restaurant where I worked, which was a blessing in itself. Although we worked all the time and never really had any extra money, we were happy. Our daughter was healthy, smart, and loving, and that's all we could ask for. The ring I bought for Michele was inexpensive, but she didn't care about that, she cared for the way I felt about her. Listen, fellas – money isn't everything, and it never will be. Don't be fooled by the glitz and glamour of Instagram celebs, media, and celebrities. People all around the world who have everything lose it all because they aren't happy. I'm not saying don't work and don't make money to survive and to take care of yourself and your family. I'm saying that you don't have to be rich or have a lot money to do so.

Live within your means. Don't buy a house, car, or clothing you can't afford. Buy things that are reasonably in your budget. Use your morality to make the best decision for yourself and family; always think about your family first, always make them a priority. Don't be that guy who buys a $1,200 watch, then can't afford to buy his kids school supplies. Now, if you don't have much money left over after paying bills, that's different. Paying BILLS is necessary for life; things like water and electricity are vital for modern living. Buying a $1,200 watch is not a necessity and should never be. Make sure you always think about how much you are spending and what you are spending it on. As my dad used to say to me, "Kelvin, it's never about the car. It's about the person that's up in it!"

It will not end up being about what kind of car you drove, what kind of watch you had, or any of that. It will always be about your character, what you stand for, what you do for others, and how you help your family. That's the real wealth. Green paper can't bring our loved ones back, green paper can't make us happy, and green paper damn sure can't ensure your health. Remember there was no amount of money in the world that could save Steve Jobs from passing, it is what it is. Use money for what it is for, buy things that you need and to help your family survive. That's it. All the extra stuff will come later in life, I promise. Just work hard, keep your head up, and continue to do well. Good things come to those who wait. Trust me, I'm a walking testimonial. I didn't get my first professional job utilizing my degree until almost three years after graduating from college. My wife, daughter, and I lived in a cottage for almost four years before we bought a house. Time is precious, it lays the foundation for how we prosper in this life. Something that may have taken the same couple with the same circumstances less time to accomplish doesn't make our journey any less right. It's unique to who you are, I wouldn't want it any other way.

I loved the struggle of grinding those long hours on my feet. They make me appreciate all the times I sit now. The older I grow, the more I am in touch with my morality, with always being conscious of the right choice to make in this life. As we see on the news daily, one bad decision can ruin your career, life, and character. It's important to always try and choose to do the right thing, even if you don't want to. Doing what's right may not always be easy, but it's right, and that's all that matters. This life is filled with opportunities and choices. You must choose the right options to set up those opportunities for yourself. It all comes full circle, you see. Like Mufasa said in *The Lion King*, this is the circle of life.

#EFFYOURBEAUTYSTANDARDS

Clothing has sizes, but style does not!

Chapter 11

First Time Fatherhood

"I cannot think of any need in childhood as strong as the need for a father's protection."

– Sigmund Freud

There is a first time for everything in this life. Being a father for the first time can be happy, scary, and exciting all at the same time. I became a first time father at 23 with my then girlfriend, now wife Michele. We were still in college when she became pregnant, and we really had no direction in terms of where we were going in life. We had to figure it out sooner or later, because this baby was coming whether we were ready or not. I found out Michele was pregnant the morning after I had partied so hard the night before that I had lost my wallet. Yeah, that's right. We all went out like college students usually do: we day drank, got wasted, drank some more, then went out and partied. I got a phone call from my dad asking me where I was the next morning. He had received a phone call from a lady who had found my wallet. Luckily for me, my dad's business card was in my collegiate canvas Velcro wallet (so lame). So the person who discovered it gave my dad her information, and he passed it along to me. I made contact with her to arrange a place and time to pick up my wallet. We agreed on that morning at a nearby gas station.

Michele and I had talked briefly about her taking a pregnancy test to find out if she was pregnant because she had missed her period. While I was away getting my wallet, she took the pregnancy test and left the results in the bathroom. When I returned to my apartment after retrieving my wallet, I saw a ghost-like look on her face as she lay in my bed. I asked her if everything was okay, and she replied, "Go look in the bathroom." I went to look and saw a pregnancy test….I came out of the bathroom holding it and asked her, "What do these lines mean?" Michele told me, "I'm pregnant!"

It felt like it was in slow motion. I replayed it a few times in my head, trying to swallow the words she had just fed me. I was a 23 year old fifth year senior in college, and I was scared shitless. I know she was too. I had to keep my composure for her sake and mine as well. I sat on the bed and we talked about the possibilities, what we both wanted, and more. It was a good conversation that I encourage all couples who are unexpectedly having children to have. We didn't plan for this to happen, but you know what they say, "When you commit the act, you run a risk of all possibilities, including pregnancy." Nonetheless, the news of being a father made me very happy. I was going to be a DAD! I was going to be someone's father, and they were going to love me forever. After the initial emotions passed through, then reality started to sink in. Were we going to be able to graduate on time? Would we have enough money to raise this child? Where were we going to live? And so forth. As the summer came to a close, we decided to move in together and be a family. We went hunting for a house to rent and found some reasonable prospects, but the majority of them didn't have good ventilation. They were also too expensive for not much house at all. We knew what we could and couldn't afford, and $800 a month in rent was unfeasible at the time for two college students about to become first-time parents.

Luckily, we found a small 500 square foot cottage. What made our living there so much more hilarious was the fact that when we first went to visit the cottage we burst out in laughter because it looked like something a leprechaun would live in! It was small, very small; so small that everything was literally one room. The kitchen, living room, and bedroom were pretty much all open. The bathroom had a door, so did the bedroom, but it wasn't much space for us to grow. In the three years of living there, we quickly outgrew that place, but we shared many memories in that cottage. I really found myself as a Dad there. I don't believe anyone is born knowing how to be a parent, it's something that just happens. You have to learn and adapt to your circumstances. I wish I could give you guidelines on how to be a perfect Dad, but I can't. I can tell you how to be loving, caring, and open-minded, because parenting involves all of the above. No two children are alike, and that's the way it's intended.

I remember when we were first responding to the pregnancy and other people kept giving us unwanted advice on how to be parents. I was 23 when I became a father; yes, I was scared, but I was also ready to take on the challenge of being an active, loving father. As we all know, most men struck with similar circumstances might bail out on their kids and leave the mother to raise the child by herself. You may not want to hear this, but I'm a firm believer in equality;

if a woman were to neglect her child after giving birth, she would be reprimanded heavily. She would probably face some charges and possible jail time. Honestly, I think the same thing should happen to men. If you choose to neglect your children and not raise them, then you should be held liable the same way a mother would...I know there are various situations, I understand that. We can't control what others do or say to us, but you can control how you pursue parenting. We have too many children in this country growing up fatherless. We need fathers the same way we need mothers.

You shouldn't get an award for staying around and being a father, it should be expected. When the expectations are clear, then they're usually met. In this modern day, so many women already expect men to be deadbeats because they have probably seen it happen too many times to others in their life. You can't blame them for thinking that – it's our duty as men to change the stereotype and enhance the expectation. We all must learn to be better while continuing to grow. Listen, I had never made a formula bottle before, I had to learn! Thank God my wife had enough intuition to show me how to make a bottle correctly. Truth be told, there was a time when I accidentally starved my daughter for a day. I wasn't mixing the right amount of formula and water together. I'm sure I'm not the only guy who has done this. As I mentioned before, we were very poor when we had Temperance, we were on Medicaid while working dead-end jobs and all. Well, I wanted to try and help us save money on formula, so that day I was literally rationing out the formula one scoop to like 12 ounces of water. My wife was at work for the day, so I was on Dad duty all day. It was one of my favorite times as a young father. You get to bond with your creation one-on-one and show them the uncondishy love you have for them. We played and I read her books, changed her diaper, fed her, and put her down for a nap. All was going very smoothly for me for my first time being Dad alone.

After she took a nap for a while, she woke up crying dramatically! I rushed into the bedroom like a superhero (just call me "Captain Save A Child"), and I realized she was probably hungry, so I made her my special "rationed saving money on formula" bottle. After she was done eating, I burped her; she started to smile and played with my face. But after about 30 minutes went by, she started crying again. I tried rocking her, but it didn't work. I tried giving her a passy (pacifier), and that didn't work either. I was about to panic, because I was running out of options! I checked her diaper to see if she was wet or had pooped – it was drier than a desert. I figured she was hungry again, so I made her another one of my special bottles; she chugged it down like she was starving. Granted, she was – later when my wife got home from work, I told her about my secret bottle-making magic, and she just looked at me like I was an idiot. I was confused, because the whole time I was thinking, "I'm doing us a favor. Saving us money on formula by rationing it out." She looked at me, smiled, and said, "Let me see you make the bottle!"

This was my time to shine as a new dad, y'all – or at least I thought it was. I grabbed the clean bottle and filled it up with 12 ounces of purified water from Publix (we might have been poor, but our Publix water made me feel bougie) and one scoop of formula. I put the nipple on and shook it up real good, and then I looked at my wife and said, "Look how much money we can save if we just ration it?" There was a pause for about 30 seconds, and then she schooled me like any mother would do on how formula is not like a Crystal Light packet. And you can't just add water in all kinds of amounts to level out the taste. If the crying Jordan face could be inserted in reality, that would have been the moment to throw it on me with the caption "BRUH" on the top of the meme. I felt horrible – here I had been thinking I was saving money and being thoughtful while actually I was doing the opposite. I was completely ignorant of the fact that she wasn't getting enough food. I deserved donkey of the day for that shit, y'all. Hit me with the "YEE-HAW" and then drop on the clues bomb one time for my wife, who let me know I was wrong and corrected my mistake.

I can proudly say it never happened again with either of our daughters. I was a freaking formula-making machine after that scolding. These are moments that you remember and cherish forever. Learning points – while everyone was giving me advice on how to be a father, they never told me how to make a formula bottle. That information would have been helpful, but as I said before, being a father is a LEARNING experience. You must be active to learn these kind of things. I'm sure plenty of dads have made mistakes like putting on the diapers backwards, which I never did, by the way. I always put them on correctly and quite quickly as well.

No matter what age you are, what race you are, or where you are from, nothing can prepare you for becoming a father. It's unique for every man on this earth. We all handle things differently, but we must always remember the first step to being a good father is actively putting being a father first. It's not going to be easy – fatherhood has its ups and downs (but mostly ups). It's okay to be scared; your life is going to change forever – for the better. While becoming a Dad is exciting and you'll want to talk about what that will look like, don't forget that as long as the baby is healthy, nothing else should matter. People give birth every day to stillborn children or children born with unfortunate life-altering circumstances. Always remember to be grateful for the healthy child you have, because many can't say the same. Spend time with your children, especially when they are young. Some of my most prized moments were hanging out with my parents when I was younger.

As time goes on, Temperance and Florinda will get older and become beautiful women in society. I can only hope that I am currently doing a good enough job of raising them and instilling discipline, love, and confidence in them. I want them to know there is nothing in this world they can't do. I was so lucky to witness the rise of America's first black president, and it gave me hope that I too can one day be anything I want to be. Hopefully, my daughters will eventually see a female president in their lifetime so they can have the same hope I did when Obama was elected. Speaking of Obama, can we just pause for a minute and give him a round of applause for being one of the most amazing presidents of all time? He is the true definition of class, style, manners, and body confidence; forever 44 (insert every positive emoji ever invented here).

Now that I'm a father of two beautiful girls and almost the dirty 30, I can say that fatherhood has changed me for the better in every way possible. It has opened my eyes to a whole new perspective on life. I have gained more patience, love, and pride in these years than I have in my entire previous life. You see, when I decided to write this book, I wanted a written record for my daughters. I want them to read this and remember what a person should be like, and how a man or woman should treat them. Fatherhood has challenged me in ways I can't even begin to explain. It continues to challenge me daily with the emotional changes of toddler to kindergarten-age kid. Watching them grow and change is one of the most beautiful transitions life has to offer; it's like watching a rose growing from concrete. Life has obstacles, walls, and bumpy roads waiting for them, but as long as you show them the way by being a good parent, they will be unstoppable. Encourage them, love them, hug them, kiss them, talk to them, and most importantly, listen to them. None of us can be perfect parents, we weren't meant to be. You will succeed, fail, cry, laugh, and worry, but in the end it's all worth it – fatherhood is worth it. Trust me, our kids need us like school needs teachers.

8 Things All Fathers Should Know

1. What you do matters more than you will ever know. How you treat people, what you do for a living, how you love their mother, and how much you contribute to the household matter. Our kids often imitate what they see us do: if you show love, act with kindness, and teach good morals, then chances are your kids will do the same; if you do the opposite, then chances are your kids will do that as well. We are all products of our environments; make sure you provide the best and most healthy environment for your kids. As parents, we all want the best for our children, and believe it or not, it all starts with us at home. Set the right example for your children to prosper in this game of life. Set them up for success, not failure!

2. Be involved and be present. Make sure you are there for football games, swim practices, baller recitals, birthdays, and more. As a parent, being around and being active are the foundations for good parenting. They know you care when you show up for their events. Support them in everything they do. My father has always been present, he attended any and everything I was ever a part of, no matter how big or how small. He set the example and tone for how I should be a father. He still sets the tone as a grandfather; he shows up to all the family events and functions. I cannot remember him ever missing one, to be honest. Being involved, present, and supportive

is the recipe for success in our children's lives. Always remember the power you have as a parent.

3.   Adapt your parenting to your child's personality and individual behavior. I have said this a lot as a parent, but when parents try to give others advice on how to parent, it falls short. It falls short because children are special and unique in their own way. Every child needs love, consistency, and structure, but how you do it is where it matters the most. I have two daughters whose personalities are VERY different. The discipline techniques that worked with our first daughter DON'T work with our second daughter. THAT"S OKAY, you have to change and adapt your parenting style. I know it's very hard to do it, but the only way to be an effective parent is to customize your parenting. Pay close attention to your child's habits, personality traits, and patterns. This will give you all the information you need to be the best father you can be to each child.

4.   Establish, set, and follow through with the rules. This is vital to being an effective parent. Rules and laws are the way of life, without them we would live in pure chaos. Some may argue we live in chaos anyway, but imagine the amount of HELL we would be in if we had no rules or laws. Rules help maintain structure and order in a good way. It's important to establish and set these in your household. That way, your children always know there is a rule, and that if they break it, there is a consequence.

5. Be consistent with parenting. If you tell your child that they can't watch their favorite show because of their misbehavior, then you have to stay consistent. Don't let them get you to be a pushover. I know it may sound silly, but kids like to take advantage and see how far they can push the envelope sometimes. A great way to nip that in the bud is to be and stay consistent about your rules, consequences, and actions. Always remember you are the adult, you are in charge, and you know what is best for your child!

6. Foster your child's independence! Let them do some things without your help; the whole idea of parenting is to raise someone to be eventually independent enough to care for him or herself. Teach them how to cook, iron, do laundry, clean, and more. I mean honestly, as a parent, I can't wait for the day where I don't have to wipe anyone else's ass but my own again. It's okay for your child to want to do things independently, don't shut them down. Chances are they have been watching you do it and want to imitate you. Watch them do it, monitor them, and correct and help them if they need it. My grandma taught me how to cook bacon, eggs, grits, and toast when I was nine. It helped me be more independent and fostered the desire to cook for others and for myself. Celebrate their independence when they accomplish something without your help. This will help them know what they are doing is right and that you SUPPORT them!

7. Expose your children to a variety of cultures. Take them places and let them try food from different

parts of the world. Teaching in the inner city, I have encountered plenty of parents and students who don't know much about the world. It's not good to be uncultured and closed-minded. We need to create more opportunities for our children to see different parts of our country and world. It's crazy to think about it, but I know kids who are 18 years old who have never been to a beach or outside of the state they live in. I travel often with my kids; I know how important it was for my sister and me to interact with people from other places as children. It helps you have a better understanding of the world, and makes you more open-minded and less ignorant of certain things. As a parent, make sure you take your kids places like the local Latin festival, black history play, the beach, a farmers' market, or even to a library. Just make sure they get out and have more of an experience than what is around them 24/7. Create a healthy environment for your children. SET THEM UP FOR SUCCESS!

8. Love them UNCONDISHY. You can never be too loving. You need to understand that a father's love is nurturing, it makes the best moments better and the worst moments okay. A father's unconditional love is like food for the soul. A child needs it to grow a healthy spirit. Kiss your kids, hug them, play with them, spend time with them, and most importantly, support them. My father disciplined me, taught me, raised me, loved me unconditionally, and helped me become the man I am now. Without him, I

wouldn't be half the man I am today. He showed me uncondishy love in every way possible. I have never doubted his love or support in my entire 30 years of living. He's been the best father any boy could ask for. As we continue to strive to be better fathers, let's remember that showing LOVE is the manliest thing we can do. Real men LOVE CONDISHY!

I'm a black, bald, bearded, brawny, beautiful, and body effing positive gentleman! #Facts

Today's leather forecast is black with a 90% chance of style

Chapter 12

Managing Your Time

"Instead of saying I don't have time, try saying it's not a priority, and see how that feels."

– Unknown

My grandmother always tells me that an idle mind is nothing but the devil's workshop. When people get bored or don't have much to do, they are more susceptible to committing senseless acts. One of the many jobs I have is being a middle school art educator, so I can tell you from my own personal experience that when students are bored, they will do stupid things. I have had students poke others with a pencil, staple the skin on their hands, put glue in their hair, and all kinds of stuff. These are all senseless acts they committed during class time because they were bored at the moment. Listen, the attention span of a middle school student is pretty much nonexistent the majority of time. So they can easily get bored or sidetracked; it happens often. I can honestly say I used to draw cartoons in class all day long. Teachers continuously called my parents about me not "paying attention" in class. Truth be told, I found drawing Beavis and Butthead more interesting than learning how to type (although I'm ironically now sitting here typing my first book). All in all, I had to learn how to multitask and figure out when to do or not do certain things. I quickly learned after the few spankings I got to pay attention in class and draw during downtime or art class.

Learning how to multitask when I was young helped me a ton as I got older. Now, at thirty I am an art educator, head football coach, model, blogger, activist, husband, father, and now author! Yes, that's nine ongoing jobs I do. It's good to stay busy, I always have something to look forward to. The good thing about these jobs is that they are all separate the majority of the time. When I wake up, I'm a husband and father, I shower, then brush my teeth and proceed to get ready to go to work. I take my youngest daughter (Florinda) to daycare every morning on my way to work. She's two right now and is absolutely precious, she's like a little Notoriously Dapper mini-me, but the female version (call her Notoriously Dainty). She makes the same faces I do and occasionally loves hats, stylish hats at that.

I'm always a father and husband, all day, every day, there are no days off from that. To me, those are the most important jobs I will ever have, always. Family is always number one – without them, we ain't shit, fellas. You know it, I know it......the world knows it. One of the most important time-management skills you need is the ability to complete the necessary tasks first. It's necessary for you to be an active husband and father, so always complete that job first. Don't try to do everything at once, I mean how crazy would it be if I was teaching art, writing my book, and attempting to coach a football team of 45-plus male adolescents all at the same physical time. It would be IMPOSSIBLE! Thankfully, my jobs can and do have their own times of day in my life.

As my students say, I'm a teacher by day and a fashion superhero by night. What's good about being a head football coach is that it's seasonal work, especially at the middle school level – at the high school level, not so much. I knew when I took on the job of being a head coach the amount of dedication, work, and patience it would take. I can admit that my first year doing it I felt overstressed; it felt like I had overbooked myself for more than what I could accomplish. You see, I teach in the inner city of Columbia, SC, and some days, teaching is more frustrating than it is fun. Coaching was just the same my first year, when I was getting used to being a young head coach with assistant coaches who were literally old enough to be my father, and trying to remain professional while being cursed out by parents because their kid didn't play in the game due to failing grades, missing practice, and behavior issues. These are things for which the education program did not prepare me. Unfortunately, you can't teach these things. You have to learn them on your own by adapting to the environment you're in.

I quickly learned how to handle certain situations at my school. If I hadn't, I probably would be REALLY stressed out and simply hating my life. Teaching is not for the fainthearted, especially in this day and age, where students can call you a "bald headed motherfucker" and not receive any punishment as a result. You can't get a phone call back from a parent when you try to reach out to them, but as soon as their child gets reprimanded for something, they are front and center at the school ready to go toe-to-toe with you. I grew up in a time (which was not that long ago) when my parents never questioned my teachers, ever. They knew I would lie to get out of trouble. They also knew that teachers had so much better things to do than just hang around to call parents and make up stories about their child's misbehavior in class.

While being a father and husband can be demanding, being a teacher can drain the living hell out of you. We are underpaid, magical, super smart babysitters essentially. We work all the time trying to improve our classroom instruction, along with mentoring students to constantly do the right thing. I mean, do you know how draining it is to say "sit down" about 2 million times a week? Teaching can be just as rewarding sometimes though, like that moment when everything gels, with every student listening and completing their assignments. It's like watching the stars align and a solar eclipse at the same time, just magical rare shit that occurs out of nowhere. If you're an educator or have worked in a school, then you know what I'm talking about. When I'm a teacher, that's what I do, I teach. I'm not thinking about football, blogging, or any of the million other things I do. When you devote your full attention to the task at hand, it's a lot easier to get it done effectively while not becoming overwhelmed. That's vital, because becoming overwhelmed can throw you off and negatively affect your performance. Doing these different jobs sometimes makes me feel like I have multiple personalities. Each one requires a different side of my personality. When I coach, the no-bullshit, strong, down set hut side comes out of me; meanwhile, when I'm blogging, the dapper, funny, gentlemanly side of me comes out.

Being able to not only multitask but actively play the required role in each of these positions takes talent. Not everyone can be a husband, father, blogger, model, activist, teacher, coach, and author. It takes special people to do those things, that's why I was chosen to do them. I'm a firm believer in trusting the process and the plan set for us. There is a reason why I teach, coach, and blog. I mean honestly, what I express in my blog is what I preach to my young men every day during school. Pull your pants up, have manners, don't talk back, stay positive, and love yourself. I actually live this lifestyle; it's not a gimmick. I practice what I preach. Living Notoriously Dapper is what I do when I teach, coach, blog, write, and advocate. All these jobs contain the same ingredients, they just are bought from different stores, you know.

I had to learn how to say no to certain things. Sometimes taking in more than you can chew is not a good thing. If taking on a task is going to make you more stressed or make your other jobs ineffective, then it's in your best interest to give it a pass. Be conscious of your free time; take advantage of clearing your mind and relaxing. Sleep is important; even though during football season I don't get much at all...it is still important. If you can try to sleep seven to eight hours a night, it will help you have stamina to do those daily tasks. If you have something important like a manuscript due to your publishing company, it's best not to procrastinate. Avoid procrastinating at all costs, especially when it comes to completing multiple tasks in a day. Occasionally I work well under pressure and tend to get shit done better. Some people like myself can handle the stress of deadlines, which was one of the few things I was good at in college. There is nothing like writing an eight-page paper the night before it's due while fueled up on caffeine. I wasn't always doing this much time management in my life, I have picked up one job after the other as time has gone on. It's important to remember to always be nice while managing your time. We all have stressful lives, some more stressful than others. You can't let that get in the way of your character. Poise is everything in this life; maintain your composure and never let them see you sweat!

I remember when my blog and Instagram were finally taking off, Chubbies Shorts booked me to do a photo shoot in D.C. I flew out on a Wednesday morning at 6 a.m., got to D.C., then did the shoot all day. Then I flew back that night, landed in Columbia at about midnight, drove home, and taught the next day like nothing had happened. It was my first moment of awe; I realized, "Shit, I can do this." As time went on, I did more and more traveling and teaching. I have gotten the hang of it, and the timing always seems to be on my side. Thankfully, most of my gigs are on the weekend or towards the end of the week. I'm also lucky enough to have a principal who understands and appreciates what I do. It would be a lot harder to accomplish my goals if I didn't have the support of my colleagues. Luckily for me, they are all supportive and want to see me win. That's beautiful – believe it or not, support is everything when you are hustling to succeed. Support is the sauce and the goal is the noodle, they go hand in hand, baby...strong.

Planning is another productive skill you need to manage your time effectively. Plan out what task you are going to conquer for that day, where you want to primarily focus your energy. I plan out all my blog and Instagram posts for the week...or at least, I try to. Some weeks are more efficient than others, it is what it is. As much as we try to plan out our lives, sometimes we get a curve ball and have to improvise. Improvising is a skill that can save a task you're trying to accomplish. As I have mentioned previously, it's important to think on your feet and to be aware. The ability to find a different way to accomplish a goal is a trait that leads to endless amounts of success. When you run into a wall, you find a way around that wall – no wall is too tall or too low for you to get through, always remember that. My third year of coaching in middle school was the best football season they had ever had since the early 2000's; we had a winning season and made it to the semifinal round of the playoffs. Tons of improvising went into that winning season, "monitor and adjust" was our watchword. We did well as coaches and as players, it was a team effort. Teamwork makes the dream work, never forget that.

8 Ways to Improve Your Time Management

1. Prioritize which tasks to complete based on importance or time required. It's best to complete something important or that takes a lot of time sooner. That way, you can use the remainder of your

energy and time completing the shorter and easier tasks of the day.

2. Be self-aware enough to know when and where you need to monitor and adjust your time. We all could be spending less or more time doing something in our lives. One of our most precious assets is time. When you're aware of what your time is being used for, you are more able to use it wisely.

3. Planning is good for those with a lot going on or for people who get overwhelmed easily. When you have your tasks planned out for the day, it's easier to get them accomplished. Make a plan, stick to it, then go after it!

4. Think on your feet, although planning is a good practice. We can never have perfect plans, right? So you need to know how to improvise. Improvising allows you to have more options when trying to finish a task. Always think of more than one way to complete something. As the old saying goes, "Work smarter, not harder"!

5. Make time for rest. Look, you can only do what your brain and body allow you to do. Without the right amount of rest, you can run the risk of exhausting yourself to the point of task destruction. You don't have to get A LOT of sleep, but try to get at least seven to eight hours a night. Your brain and body will then be prepared to take on your most daunting task of the day.

6. Avoid procrastination as much as possible – putting things off to the last minute can cause more anxiety than expected. We have all had those "I have a million things to do" type of days. Most of the time, when we think of what we have to get done, the majority of the tasks are things we have put to the side and waited until the last minute to do. Planning and improvising help eliminate the possibility of procrastination.

7. Take advantage of your free time! When I have free time, I try to grab a coffee or do something enjoyable. Free time is a great time for us to do the things we WANT to do, things unrelated to work or school. Most people pick up a hobby in their free time to make up for their stressful work week.

8. Learn to say "no" to certain things. As an art teacher, I get asked to make plenty of signs or anything decorative. Sometimes, if I already have too much on my plate, I say no. I have to, we all have had tasks that we pick up and later realize we shouldn't have. I can count on about a hundred fingers and toes the amount of times I have regretted taking on an extra task. Don't add things to your life that are going to stress you or make it harder for you to accomplish your goal.

All white. No privilege. #ModernGentleman

I feel like money when I make a change

They say you are what you eat. If that's the case, I'd be sweet!

Chapter 13

Family Affairs

"Black excellence, opulence, decadence."

– Jay-Z

One of the many things we can't choose in life is the family we are born into. As an educator, I have encountered students with various kinds of home lives. Some people are lucky and are born into a family that loves them, shows them the way to behave, and most importantly, teaches them to be a good person. Others are not so lucky; the older I've gotten, the more people I've met with dysfunctional families. I was fortunate enough to be raised without dysfunction in my family. So naturally, when I met others who didn't have a close relationship with their parents, I was taken aback. How can someone not talk to his or her parents? How can a parent not talk to their child? It was something I had to learn about on a friend-to-friend basis. For some reason, a lot of my past relationships consisted of girls who had "daddy issues". It was a strange thing for me to date someone who didn't talk to their dad or wanted nothing to do with their dad for various reasons. I started to notice after about my second serious girlfriend why these types of girls were attracted to me. I was the good guy, the one who opened the door, told them they were beautiful, paid attention to them, and listened to what they had to say. My parents raised me to be that way. It was just natural for me to be a nice guy. But because I was nice, I would get hurt; as my grandmother says, "Hurt people simply hurt people." I didn't fully grasp that concept until I dated this girl named Jess.

She had a terrible relationship with her parents, so bad that they kicked her out of their house for dating me. Since I come from a family that is open-minded and always willing to help others, they took Jess in without a question and gave her the option to stay with us until things settled down with her family. My parents didn't have to do this; they weren't required to offer her a place to stay, but they did. Jess stayed with us for about a week and a half, then her dad came around and talked with her, and she decided it was best she moved back home until she graduated. We dated for about one more year, then decided to call it quits due to what happened that I described in Chapter 1 (she slept with another guy). Nonetheless, the real MVPs were my parents. The example they have shown my sister and me is reflected in us. I have two male cousins whose mother kicked them out when they turned 18, and my parents again without question took them in. Jamal is the younger one of the two; we have always been close, and I pretty much consider him a brother. When he moved in with us, I was in college at the time. He was still in high school, trying to finish strong. Jamal is unique because due to not having the best circumstances in life, he always had support from my parents, my grandmother, and my Auntie Charlene. He was always determined to make it no matter what he was faced with. His poise reminded me of all the people in my family who I admire, my Dad, Mom, sister, grandmother and aunt. Poise and class is something that runs in my family's blood, you see. When I was faced with an obstacle, it was never my option to quit or stop. My only way of working through a challenge was finding a way to defeat it. That's the Davis way of thinking.

My mom has always been my number one in everything I do. When I wanted to drop out of college because I was burned out, she quickly let me know that wasn't an option. Momma don't take no messing around. She is loving, rational, and brilliant, the definition of class and being a lady. I get the majority of my confidence from my mother. She always instilled that in me; I have never been afraid to go after my dreams or something I want in life because of the way she taught me to be resilient. Thanks to her, I like being told "no" – it gives me fuel to keep going and pursue my passion. Modeling agencies have told me "no" left and right; did that stop me from making a name for myself? No. If I had listened to what they said, then I wouldn't have become Notoriously Dapper. I wouldn't have been nominated for Yahoo's Diversity in Beauty "model activist of the year" award. It's because of that determination – my mom gets all the glory. When I'm down, she picks me up, that's what mothers do. They nurture us, they discipline us, and they define us. We are a product of our environments; what I am today is based on the environment my parents created for me. They are loving, tolerant, thoughtful, aware, understanding, and kind. My dad, aka "the definition of being a gentleman", is everything I want and wish to be. He has worked in law enforcement for 20-plus years. He is now a chief of police and a constant reminder of the good cops who work every day to help save lives in our community.

Being a black man, my dad had that conversation with me when I started driving; you know, that 'what to do when you get pulled over by a cop' talk. Every black teenager can relate to this conversation, and let's face it – this conversation is a lot different for white families. When I got my license and starting driving to school, I knew I was going to get pulled over eventually. Black male teen driving a Mercedes in white suburbia equals sirens all day. What was different for me was coming home to face another police officer after I got my speeding tickets. My father always warned me about speeding, playing my music too loud, and not wearing my seat belt. He would often tell me that these are reasons why you could get stopped, and when you do get stopped, be polite, refer to them as 'officer', and always be attentive. I always followed these protocols when getting pulled over; sometimes I would get a ticket and sometimes I wouldn't.

I never really felt like I was being profiled when I got pulled over until I was 23. Because I was getting a fair amount of speeding tickets and being a typical teen driver, my parents decided it was best that I didn't have a car after my freshman year of college. For almost four years I didn't have a car – rightfully so. I needed to learn more responsibility. My parents would let me borrow their car every now and then to run errands. When I became a father, fortunately, my Aunt Charlene gave me her old Volvo. This was the car I used to go to work and travel to my schools for student teaching. After years of not having a car, I learned to be responsible and not take having a car for granted. I was grateful and felt really blessed to have a second chance at having my own car. I drove the speed limit, wore my seatbelt, and didn't play any music because the car had no radio.

After I graduated from college, I was clearly in the market to get a "big boy" job to support my new family. After driving home from an interview one day, I got pulled over in my neighborhood as I approached a stop sign on my street. The cops were two young white males. They drove past me and signaled for me to pull over, so I did. They got out of the police car, and one approached the driver's side while the other approached the passenger side; then they asked where I was headed. I replied that I was going home (my house was a block away from where they pulled me over), and they asked to see my license and registration. I gave it to them; then after they walked off, I called my father. He instructed me to ask them why they had pulled me over and to keep him on the phone.

They came back and asked me for my proof of insurance. I then asked, "Why am I being stopped, officer?" They told me there had been a lot of break-ins in the area lately and that I looked like I was up to some suspicious activity. Mind you, I had a mint green shirt, pink tie, and grey suit on, since I had just come from a job interview. Looking confused and telling them where I lived meant nothing to them. I started looking for my insurance card and couldn't find it. I asked if I could show them electronically, and they said no. They then asked me to step out of my car. They searched me and my car and clearly found nothing. So they gave me a ticket for no proof of insurance. I asked them. "Why did I get pulled over? How do I look suspicious in a shirt and tie? Why can't I show you my insurance card on my phone?" They told me, "Be glad we only gave you a ticket for no proof of insurance." I knew after that it was best for me to take the ticket and move on. I called my father back afterwards and explained what had happened. After explaining to him that I felt racially profiled and that I was pulled over because I "looked suspicious", he helped me file the proper paperwork to seek some type of justice. But as usual nothing happened, and my complaint went unnoticed, I assume.

As time went on and I saw more headlines of unarmed black men being killed, I couldn't help but think about that situation. I kept replaying it in my head over and over again. I could easily have become a victim of police brutality that day, but I didn't. Other people can't say the same. During the heat of all this tension between cops and civilians, I had to reach out to my dad. I reminded him of that story and told him how unsafe I felt without my wife and girls around. I told him that I feel as though I'm valued and seen as nothing but a threat when I'm by myself. When I'm with my family, I feel as though people perceive me as less of a threat. He listened, he heard me, and most of all, he understood how I felt. You see, I know there are good and bad people in every profession. I can't hate cops, because I was raised by one of the greatest cops of all time. Not many people are great at what they do, but he is. My dad is the example of what law enforcement should be: there to protect ALL citizens no matter where they live or what they look like. He's been in law enforcement 20-plus years and has never shot or killed anyone. While unfortunately there are bad officers out there, we can let the small number of bad cops outweigh the good. I just hope one day all police officers can be as thoughtful of the citizens they are sworn to protect as he is.

Racism is real. Bigotry is real. Misogyny is real. Homophobia is real. I know it's real, I've seen it. I've seen others experience it throughout my life. One person who knows all of these too well is my sister Courtney. She's a proud gay black woman. While I only have to deal with racism and bigotry, she has to deal with all four. Growing up, Courtney was my right-hand man. We liked to do everything together when we were younger. We would play outside for hours. We loved playing Mortal Kombat, watching wrestling, and arguing with one another. What brothers and sisters don't argue, right? Especially when it's Palmetto Bowl time? Courtney is a Clemson graduate and needless to say a Clemson fanatic (and rightfully so). I went to Carolina, so naturally our parents' house is divided. But as my mom says, it doesn't matter who wins, because those checks cleared to send us both through school. One of these days Carolina will be back on top in football, but for now I will settle for a girls' Gamecocks basketball championship and a Tigers football championship. Regardless of who you root for, no one can deny that our state has collegiate sports on lockdown! Baseball, football, and basketball – I'll take it.

I know what it's like to be black; I know how it feels to have your skin tone be viewed as a dangerous weapon. I don't know what it's like to be gay, and I definitely have no clue what it's like to be a woman. I can say that being racially discriminated against is enough. I can't imagine dealing with hate for my race, sexual orientation, and gender. But somehow Courtney has done it; she has not let any of that stop her from graduating, getting a job, earning her masters degree, marrying her partner, or buying a house. As her older and only brother, I couldn't be more proud of her. She has been through many dark places in her life, but she always finds the light and comes out shining like a diamond.

When she first came out, it was just a family secret, none of our extended family knew. I bet it was hard for her to keep that a secret from them, especially from our grandma. You can't hide it forever! Eventually it came out, and now the whole family knows. After all, she and her wife are married and bought a house together. When they invited us to their housewarming party, it was amazing to see the amount of love and support they had. People of all ages, races, and backgrounds all came together to celebrate them and their new house. It was honestly one of the most beautiful things I have seen. People in our family had some homophobic views, but when they found out Courtney was gay, it changed them for the better. As my dad says, whatever you hate will end up in your family and you will be forced to love it. If that ain't the truth, then I don't know what is!

Family should always come first. They need you just as much as you need them. I'm so thankful to have parents who love me unconditionally and who forgive me for tearing up their three Mercedes. I know when my girls get older, karma is going to pay me a little visit or two. When it does, I will know how to handle the situation, thanks to my parents. As a black family of four living in white suburbia, we always stayed woke. My parents always looked out for our best interests and provided us with anything we needed to prosper in life. We knew we had to work for everything we had, our parents made sure that we didn't get any handouts. That's why my sister and I are so successful in what we do. We know we have to go get it. If we want it, we will achieve it. I want to thank my parents and sister for dealing with me during my own dark times, times of anger, anxiety, and sadness. Thank you for never turning your back on me and for loving me unconditionally. I will never forget you spending your savings to send me to Italy to study oil painting (one of the greatest moments of my life).

The older I've gotten, the more I've realized the love we share as a family is rare. I can only hope to one day be as great a parent as they are. As a young father, I learn every day; I take mental notes from what you've given me and apply it to my own parenting. I want my kids to not be afraid of who they are. My parents taught Courtney and me to follow our dreams and own who we are. As we continue to do that in our daily lives, we live through all the values and principles you instilled in us. We live with love, tolerance, understanding, awareness, and kindness.

Black excellence, truly yours.

LOVE THE SHIT OUT OF YOURSELF! #JustDoIt

Yeezy like Sunday Morning.

Chapter 14

Infidelity: How to Prevent and Deal

"You almost went Eric Benét. Let the baddest girl in the world get away, I don't even know what else to say. Never go Eric Benét."

– Jay-Z

There's really no right or wrong way for me to approach this topic. Infidelity happens every day; I want to put a spotlight on how to prevent it from occurring, and if it's already happened, how to deal with it. It's a painful, deeply personal experience that many don't feel comfortable broadcasting. When someone decides to be unfaithful in a relationship, it has nothing to do with you as the partner. It has everything to with them and their decision. Many people try to figure out why their partner was unfaithful and tend to blame themselves for it. It's a natural feeling to have for a person who has been cheated on. You ask yourself questions like, "What did I do wrong? What could I have done better? Am I not good enough?" None of these questions should ever come up, because you're never to blame. I know it's easier said than done, coming from someone who has been in that circumstance.

Everyone is unique in how they handle situations like infidelity. We've heard stories of people being killed, marriages destroyed, and even "love children". It's no secret that high profile athletes, musicians, and public figures have had affairs. We see it all the time in the media – Tiger

Woods, Kobe Bryant, Robin Thicke, and so on. Sometimes temptation gets the best of you and you make a choice, not thinking of the long-term consequences. I remember watching a docuseries on people who had survived infidelity in their marriage. This one story tugged at my heartstrings, because this guy was literally the exception as well as the example of what anyone should do in this situation. He was a pastor at a church, and he and his wife decided to take in a foreign exchange student from Africa. During the episode, this man constantly talked about his love for his family and wife. He did everything he could to make her happy; of course, to him they had a pretty stable relationship. It seemed as though he never expected his wife to cheat on him, and rightfully so, who would? As the story developed, he mentioned that he'd had a vasectomy a few years back and could no longer have children. It was a decision they had both agreed on in their marriage at the time. She said that she didn't want any more children.

The pastor continued to spread the word of positivity, while his wife, on the other hand, was sleeping with the African foreign exchange student. The student was only with them for a few months and then went back to his country. I'm watching this, saying to myself, damn, what the hell? And the plot gets thicker. Towards the end of the episode, she found out she was pregnant. Obviously, the pastor was a little taken aback by it, but he put his faith in God. He said, "It was a miracle. God wanted us to have more children." Meanwhile, the wife knew she was pregnant by the African exchange student and was in too deep to get an abortion, not that they believed in that anyhow. The whole time I was watching this, thinking how this poor dude thinks he's having a miracle child, and really his wife cheated on him. I was like damn, this is some fucked up shit. I'm thinking she's got to tell him before she gives birth! But she didn't, this dude went through the whole pregnancy thinking it was his miracle child. Then she gave birth, and clearly something wasn't right – the baby was half black. After a few days in the hospital, she confessed to him what she did, then the show cut to the commercial break. I was like, NOOOOOOO! I was on the edge of my seat waiting to see what happened next, what was he going to say? Did he flip out in the hospital? Did he find forgiveness in him and move on?

It came back on and showed a reenactment of his reaction. This man was calm and so understanding. She was crying and bawling, confessing to her faults – she understood that her marriage could be over. She thought her family was ruined. In most circumstances it would have been, that's why this guy was the exception. He accepted the situation but knew there was not much he could do. He talked about how at first he was fueled with anger and wanted nothing to do with the child or her. Her children were obviously astonished as well. I mean, it tore this family apart, but he realized that the only one who was going to suffer was the child. He knew the African exchange student was gone and was not going to be an active father; hell, the student probably didn't know he got her pregnant. This man not only forgave his wife while starting the healing process to fix what she had done, but he decided to raise the child as his OWN!

Y'all, I started crying. I couldn't help but think about how mad I would be and how betrayed I would feel in that circumstance, but that's what makes us unique. He found the positive in the situation and became a new father all over again. It showed home videos of the child's birthday parties, starting school, and all. I couldn't believe this man didn't leave his wife but decided to stay and raise that child. Honestly, who can say they would do the same? I can't. He is the example of what a gentleman does when being faced with such daunting circumstances. He did nothing wrong! She cheated on him, got pregnant, and lied to him – and he owned it. I mean, it takes a lot to do what he did. It takes even more to speak publicly about it, especially to the world on a broadcast TV network. Their story probably helped save a lot of marriages. It put it in perspective and made people start to think, "If he can do it, why can't I?" I applaud him for his reaction, having enough guts to claim and raise that boy as his son.

He thought about the long-term effects of her infidelity, and he knew that child would have suffered for no reason at all. He saw the bigger picture – he was selfless. Infidelity is wrong. There is no way around it; no one should cheat on his or her spouse. If you're unhappy, vocalize that, go to counseling, and work on the issues you all have. When all else fails, then you should decide to move on from the relationship, whether that involves separation or divorce. Sometimes things just don't work out, that doesn't mean it's the end of the world. Life continues, and you need to move along with it. Most people who have dealt with an unfaithful partner don't have the happy ending that the pastor and his wife had. Each person is different. I have always believed in not judging people's reactions to someone else's actions. We are all human, we make mistakes...we are perfectly imperfect. The way another person handles something isn't going to be the same way you may handle it. I do think we can all learn from other people's mistakes, actions, and stories though. I know I have, a lot of mistakes we don't make are due to having watched others make them. Seeing another person's consequences, actions, or circumstances can help us make better decisions in our lives. That's what life is all about, mental, emotional, and spiritual growth.

I'm not saying we all need to act like the pastor when faced with situations like that, but he is a great example of how to deal with it. When my girlfriend of two years cheated on me...I really felt it. I was hurt, lost, and angry, but like everything else in life, you have to move on. People are going to do what they want to do, don't try to control another individual. It's not healthy for you or them. People should live freely and make the right decisions in their life. If they choose not to, then it is their issue, not yours. I believe there are ways to prevent making bad decisions like infidelity. Emphasizing love and attention can help prevent infidelity on both ends. When you show your partner love and attention, they are less likely to seek to find it elsewhere. You are also satisfying your own need for love and attention by doing so.

Ignoring temptation is another way to prevent being unfaithful, though it can be hard to ignore. It's important to think about the long-term effects your actions may have.

You don't want to ruin your family over something that is meaningless, let's be honest – you don't want to ruin your family over anything! Family is everything. Stay focused on your goals in life. Staying busy can also help prevent infidelity. When your mind is preoccupied with doing other tasks, then you don't have time to worry about anything else. Increasing your partner's motivation and desire to stay with you is the best way to keep them faithful. Show your partner that you love and care for them. Raise your level of romance to keep their attention, try out a new outfit or maybe even a romantic date. Reward your partner for what they do for you and attend to their need for romance, especially sex. These methods will help keep them and you from wandering while also making your relationship more fulfilling.

We all dream of being married forever like our grandparents were. I'm sure many of them were unfaithful or did things many would disapprove of, but they worked on issues. They talked to each other, not at each other. I saw a quote from a couple who had been married for 50-plus years, someone asked them how they made their marriage last. They replied, "We come from a generation where when something is broken, we fix it. We don't throw it away and get something new." If we all had that mentality, then I think our lives would be a lot easier. We are so quick to give up on people and move on. Working on your relationship or marriage is a good thing, it shows you care about improving the foundation you all have built. When faced with an unfaithful partner, you have a decision to make, whether to deal with it or leave. Considering the divorce rate is 50 percent, I think it's safe to say half stay and half leave. I believe the first step to healing is facing the problem. When you face a problem, you are forced to find some sort of solution.

Dealing with infidelity is not easy, and there is no textbook way to handle it, but there are methods to help you cope. Talking to someone you trust about it is where good friends come into play. When you're faced with something like this, you don't need people telling you what to do, you need someone to listen to you. Don't jump to conclusions and make up scenarios that aren't true, it will drive you crazy and put you in a toxic state mentally. Instead, reflect on the information you know. Take time to think about it and what you want to do next in your relationship. You know what is best for you and your situation.

This topic is very taboo, and to be honest, it is hard to bring it to a conclusion. All in all, from my personal experience with an unfaithful partner, I think assessing the circumstances on an individual basis is what's best. As I said before, cheating is wrong. I strongly suggest that no one do it at all. That's the easiest way to prevent it. If it doesn't occur, then you don't have to face it, it's that simple. Be faithful to your partner, love them, care for them, attend to their needs, kiss them, hug them, and most importantly make them feel special. Buy flowers for your partner every once in a while, write them a note, or spice it up in the bedroom with them. Whatever you do, just make sure you put effort into your marriage. Just because you married them doesn't mean the romance stops. You have to continue putting in work. If you're unhappy, then let them know. Closed mouths don't get fed, always be vocal and let them know how you feel. Communication is the key to a lasting relationship. Keep your effort strong and love them uncondishy. Let this be a reminder to everyone out there reading this, you can make it last forever when you work on what is broken...don't just throw it away.

Known to give the color red the blues!

When life hands you haters, just smile at them. They really love you

I wear my heart on my sleeve like a bracelet. #LoveUncondishy

Chapter 15

Love, Laugh, and Live Your Life

"If you have the opportunity to play this game of life, you need to appreciate every moment. A lot of people don't appreciate the moment until it's passed."

– Kanye West

After reading the last 14 chapters, I hope you have gained some sort of clarity on what it takes to become your own man and to live as your own man. Becoming a man is not easy; while most people think it's a matter of age, it's not, it's a matter of maturity and life experience. It's having the right character traits to help you function well in today's modern world. Let's face it before it's too late, we live in a digital world where books, magazines, and more are at our fingertips...just a click away. So naturally, it's easy to want instant results and gratification, but that's not real life. We have to work for gratification, and you have to earn the results you want in life. Every human wakes up with the same amount of time in a day, how we choose to use that time is up to us as individuals. Over the past few years, these three elements have really helped me gain a new perspective on who I am: love, laughter, and living your own life.

Love who you are, what you do, and how you look, and those around you will follow suit. Show love whenever you get an opportunity to show it. Love comes in an array of ways and should be expressed just as diversely. Love for humanity is what is missing in this world; we are often told we can only love people we are close with. That's not true, you can love humanity and use kindness to show that love. Kindness creates an everlasting ripple that can last forever in our hearts. People never forget how you made them feel. Do what you love, our time on this earth is too limited to be stuck doing something we hate. Don't spend time trying to please others what their ideal of happiness is. You can't please everyone, but you can be nice to everyone. You will lose your own happiness and self-worth if you try to always be accepted by others. As long as you love you, then no one can take your happiness away from you. Love is such a beautiful emotion.

I first discovered the beauty of this emotion through my first love...art. Art to me is any personal expression. I remember when I found out I could draw – I was about six years old, and I drew Bugs Bunny. If I had the drawing now and compared it to my later work, I would think I was horrible at art, but in that moment, I found something I loved to do. As I mentioned earlier, I would get in trouble for drawing in the bible during church and sketching during class instead of doing assignments. When I got older, I read and learned about the history of art. It simply fascinated me how artists could depict so much emotion with line, shape, and color. I started making the correlation between fashion and art when I was about 11 years old. I realized that clothes could be used the same way any artistic medium is used. You can depict your emotion, attitude, or personality by how you dress. The color, patterns, prints, and fit you choose can play into all of this. I have always viewed the human body as a blank canvas. When people are staring at a blank canvas, they are staring at the potential of what it could become. We as people need to look at humans the same way, especially ourselves. Look at your body and see the potential you have – the potential is endless for you. You can become whatever you want, just choose your medium and start painting your potential. You see, art is in everything we do. From the cars we drive to the buildings we sit in, from the food we eat to the clothes we wear...it's all art. How can you not love art? It's what makes this world go around. Love is an art form, the art of loving others and yourself.

After you decide to do what you love, eat what you love, and wear what you love...laugh. Laugh at all the silly mistakes you made as a kid, laugh at the past relationships you had, laugh in the face of haters. Laughter is good for the soul. Laughter is more than just a sound; it's a whole body experience. When you laugh, 15 facial muscles contract while your breathing becomes more irregular; even your tear ducts can become activated ("I laughed so hard I cried"). The muscles throughout our bodies can tense up when laughter spreads from our face through our respiratory system and eventually through our entire bodies, which explains why our stomachs can hurt from laughing hard. People usually laugh because they're happy, but laughter also has the power to *make* us happy. Laughter releases endorphins that have the same effects as drugs like morphine, which are responsible for feelings of being on cloud nine. Having a good sense of humor can help enhance your ability to laugh more, which in turn will make you happier.

Sometimes we all need a good laugh. Life can be rough sometimes; it's unpredictable and unfortunately is not fair. Memes have taken over the internet in a good way – with all the negative cyberbullying out there, it's nice to have things out there to smile and laugh about. My favorite meme to this date is the viral video of Shirley Caesar preaching about the glory of God that started the #UNAMEITCHALLENGE. In the video, a beat is pulsing, and the words on the top read, "Me: Grandma, what you cooking for Thanksgiving?" She says, "I got beans, greens, potatoes, tomatoes, lambs, rams, hogs, dogs, chicken, turkeys...YOU NAME IT!" If you have watched this and not laughed, then I don't know what to tell you. That video along with a bunch of others on the web can make your day a whole lot brighter. I'm laughing right now, cause I had to watch it after writing about it, y'all.

Lastly y'all, and yes, I say "y'all" because I'm from the South. (If you don't like it, then all y'all can close this book right now – psych! Don't do that. I need for you to hear what I have to say a little bit longer.) I want you to live your life, not to live someone else's life, but yours. As Rihanna sings in one of my favorite T.I. songs, "So live your life (Hey! Ay ay ay) You steady chasing that paper, just live your life (Oh! Ay ay ay) Ain't got no time for no haters, just live your life (Hey! Ay ay ay) No telling where it'll take ya, just live your life (Oh! Ay ay ay)" Don't live out someone else's goals and ambitions, live out *yours*. You can be great at whatever you want to be. When you live for yourself, you will feel happier about what you accomplish. Yes, you need to do things for your family. Yes, you need to make sacrifices. But that doesn't mean you can't live for yourself, because you can. Just because I'm a husband and father doesn't mean I can't pursue my goals. I'm doing it right now – I've always dreamed about writing a book on being a modern gentleman. I never thought it would be possible; I could have quit a long time ago and just taken a loss. To me, there are no losses, only learning. If you don't get what you want, that doesn't mean the road stops, that doesn't mean give up…you've got to want it as bad as you want to breathe. You've got to wake up with a mission, use your time wisely, and spread love in the process. It all circles back to love, it's the foundation of what we live on – without it, we are nothing.

I say this because I believe it: don't worry about what others do with their lives. Stay focused on *your* life and what YOU want to live for. I have a college friend who was born a male, but after finishing law school, he decided to change himself into a female. He expressed how he has always felt that he was living in the wrong body. Before he made his decision public, I remember talking with a group of friends at a wedding. The conversation was about Bruce Jenner and his transition to becoming Caitlyn. Some of our friends were opinionated and stated how disgusted they were by it and whatnot. I personally have never been worried about someone else's lifestyle unless it causes physical harm to others. When I decided to chime in and give my two cents, I said to them all, "We have to let people live their lives." We can't judge someone based on the decisions they make to better themselves. Whether he was a male or female, I was always going to treat her/him with respect. Honestly, it didn't matter to me. What matters to me is what is in your heart: are you loving? Are you nice? Are you caring? That's what should matter to people, not what you look like. We come in various sizes, colors, and ages, and we all deserve to live our lives freely.

If you're reading this and you're struggling with your identity, racial issues, relationship problems, family troubles, or anything that has you down, I want you to know this – it's only temporary and it will get better with time. To help ensure that it will get better, just keep living your life. Don't worry about the haters, racists, misogynists, or homophobes, be the best version of you every day. People love finding something to hate to help make them feel better, when in truth people who do this are insecure. Insecure people live their lives through other people's ideas, they don't think for themselves. Whatever you are, be proud of it. You're so special; there is only one of you in this world. There is a reason why no two fingerprints are identical. We each have a gift, but it's up to you to activate it and use it for good. I know I have a responsibility to share my knowledge and story with you all. That's what I signed up for when I decided to start my blog and eventually write this book. By sharing my life experiences and advice, I hope to bring more positivity to this world.

I love you all. Thank you for making this possible, this is my first book. Hopefully there will be more to come. I had no idea that by starting a body positive menswear blog I would reach so many people who struggle or have struggled with the same demons – the demons that feed into what the media and society want us to be, rather than being the best version of ourselves. Whether you're a man or woman reading this, I hope this book brings you clarification on what it takes to be a modern day gentleman or lady with style, manners, and body confidence. We need you all in this world right now more than ever. People who care. People who want better for our present and future generations. Together we can change this world for the better, one day at a time. Join me in taking the Notoriously Dapper challenge...I challenge you to love uncondishy, laugh uncontrollably, and live your life freely, with no boundaries. Be you and be confident, strong.

Love Uncondishy,
Kelvin of Notoriously Dapper

Confidence is key!

I like short shorts and I cannot lie. Those other legs can't deny! #YouKnowIt

#StyleHasNoSize

Wear what makes you happy #BeYouBeConfident

Acknowledgments

"Real recognize real."

– Project Pat

I can't believe this, y'all...I'm a published author. When I first started this book, I didn't know how to approach what I wanted to say. I had to search and find my writing voice; this was no easy task, but damn, it was worth it. These words will live with people forever, while hopefully sprinkling some positivity on this world. From style to manners and from manners to body confidence, I hope you all have enjoyed this book as much as I have enjoyed sharing my stories and advice with you all. Being a gentleman doesn't mean being perfect, it just means you're being kind, tolerant, aware, thoughtful, loving, and understanding. Keep being you while taking care of yourself and loving those around you. With that being said, I can't end this book without thanking and acknowledging the people who contributed to my life and this journey. You made this book possible!

My parents: Thank you so much for believing in me. Pushing me to be the greatest I can be at all times. Dad, thank you for showing me what it is to be a man, to take care of my family, stay humble, work hard, accept my faults, and continue to pursue my dreams. You always told me, "Son, if you like it, then I love it" – you showed that day in and day out of my life. You haven't agreed with all of the decisions I made in my life, but you have always supported me. Mom, thank you for instilling your hustler mentality in me. You push me to be more loving and to persevere through my difficult times. I am able to write this book and put myself out there in the name of self-love because of what you instilled in me. You have shown me what it truly means to be fearless. As time continues to set me on various paths in life, I remember all the positivity you gave me during difficult moments. This book wouldn't be possible without you two. Thank you, I love you.

My wife: Michele Jordan Davis, I appreciate you letting me spend those extra hours in coffee shops writing while holding down the fort at home. You are my favorite person on this earth. You complete me in ways you can't imagine. We truly are a dream team (Jordan and Pippen). You have been with me since day one of this journey, snapping photos of me whenever I needed you to, even at nine months pregnant. You are a trooper; I thank you so much for loving me and being patient with me. As many would agree, being married to me is a book in itself! It's not easy, I know, but you're there through thick and thin, better or for worse. You're my inspiration for life. Thank you for helping me as I continue to pursue my dreams. I love you, uncondishy.

My sister: Courtney, you have taught me to accept everyone no matter where they come from or what they look like. You are the true definition of love. Your heart is so big, and it warms my heart to see you show love. I'm glad you found Catie, she is lucky to have you. I think about you every day, and I often reminisce on all the fun times we had as kids. I know I wasn't the best big brother when I was in middle school. I apologize for that. Although life has taken its toll and we don't get to speak or see each other often, I want you to know that I love you with every ounce of my heart. You're beautiful, kind, loving, and truly STRONG! Thank you for your tolerance, patience, and love. You are the bomb dot damn com. No one could ask for a better little sister.... no one.

My grandmothers: The wisdom you have shared with me has helped me accumulate what is in this book. You all are fierce, classy, and the epitome of being a lady. I can't wait for you to read some of your quotes in this book. You have always known best. I love you.

My aunt Charlene: Thank you for showing me what it is to love uncondishy. You blessed me with the freshest outfits as a kid. Your style is unmatched and undefeated. You are a fighter and a champion. I love you uncondishy.

My cousin Jamal: Bro, literally that's what you are to me. Thank you for building me up on days I was down. Your life journey has inspired me to persevere through all obstacles. Nothing has ever stopped you from achieving everything you want in this life. You are the true definition of a go-getter. Keep being you, man. I love you, brother.

To my best friends: Adam, Alan, and Devon...you three are the sugar honey iced tea. Thank you for showing me what true friendship is, and for helping me find who I truly am. You all have accepted me for who I am since day one. I appreciate that. I know that life has pulled us in many directions and we don't get to talk as much, but when we do, it's like we never skipped a beat. We pick up right where we left off. As life continues to bless us and treat us well, I hope our families can grow to know the bond we all share with one another. For you all are truly my brothers from another mother. Thank you for being the best modern gentlemen around. I love you all, strong.

To Mango Publishing: Thank you to everyone over at Mango Publishing. This book became a reality because you saw something inside my message. I have always dreamed of writing a book, but never thought it was possible. Because of you, this dream has now became a reality. I can't thank you enough for providing me this opportunity with so much creative control. Brenda, I appreciate you always emailing me, giving me feedback, and providing me with motivation. Roberto, thank you for working with me on the cover, my indecisiveness was getting the best of me some days. Truth be told, this book is symbolic of what teamwork does when people from all different parts of the world work together to make something positive happen. I am honored and blessed to be a member of the Mango Publishing family. I look forward to more years to come!

To Temperance and Florinda: Being your father has given me the greatest moments of my life. These years of fatherhood have shown me what it means to be selfless, humble, and most importantly, patient. Parenting is not in a textbook; it just happens...you just do it. Watching you all grow, play, dance, sing, and learn is the most rewarding thing I can ask for. This book is for you; I want you to know how you should be treated by your partner and how you should feel about yourself. You should always love who you are and what you do. I know being girls of mixed race you will face some challenges in life, just as most people do. My job is to raise you strong enough to persevere through those obstacles and continue down your path of success. Life isn't easy, and I don't ever want you to think it is. There will be ups and downs, but always remember it's only temporary. I love you with all my heart. Loving you two unconditionally fulfills me more than anything else in this life. This second half of my book, "Living as your own man", would not have been possible without you two. You have shown me what it means to truly be a man and take care of his family. I can't imagine my life without you. May God keep blessing you with all the love in the world; I look forward to watching you grow up to be the amazing, strong, and talented women you were destined to be. Always remember, whatever you need... Dad is here for you, anytime, anywhere, any place. I got you, strong. I love you forever and always, uncondishy.